Dr Panofsky
& Mr Tarkington

Dr Panofsky
& Mr Tarkington

AN EXCHANGE OF LETTERS,

1938-1946

EDITED BY RICHARD M. LUDWIG

PRINCETON, NEW JERSEY

PRINCETON UNIVERSITY LIBRARY

1974

Published under the sponsorship of
the Friends of the Princeton University Library
Design by P. J. Conkwright
Printed in the United States of America
by Princeton University Press
at Princeton, New Jersey
Illustrations by The Meriden Gravure Company

FOR

GERDA PANOFSKY

Preface

Publishing an exchange of letters from World War II would need little explanation if the authors had been military heroes or eminent journalists, or even government officials in Washington recording their contributions to the war effort. We always want to know the intimate side of history. But this correspondence, although dated 1938-1946 and written by two eminent authors, is a remarkable collection not for its national importance but for its very opposite, for the light it throws on private lives during wartime and for its description of a somewhat improbable friendship between an elderly American popular novelist and a learned German art historian almost twenty-five years his junior. That the correspondence exists in such fullness is remarkable in itself.

Erwin Panofsky met Booth Tarkington in the summer of 1938 in Kennebunkport, Maine, a charming coastal village not far from the New Hampshire border. The permanent residents of any seaport have always made sharp distinctions between "natives" and "summer people." The Panofskys were clearly visitors to Maine, not even "summer people"; in fact, they had only recently become residents of the United States. The Tarkingtons were something more than "summer people" but not quite "natives." In any event, they were gracious hosts to the visiting scholars and the new acquaintance developed into a lengthy correspondence and repeated visits in Princeton, Indianapolis, and Philadelphia as well as Maine. The history and collecting of art may have been the subject that sparked this friendship but the presence of mutual friends, the stage both these men had reached in their careers, and the date on the calendar were other reasons for nurturing it. Had they met a decade earlier, Panofsky would have been visiting from the University of Hamburg and Tarkington preparing for eye surgery. As it was, the timing was fortuitous. But now we are ahead of the story.

Booth Tarkington made his first visit to Kennebunkport in July, 1903, little realizing it would in time become his second home. A native of Indianapolis, he had known the East from his school days at Phillips Exeter Academy and Princeton University, and from a winter in New York City trying to sell his short stories; but he never intended to be more than a visitor. He had published his first novel, *The Gentleman from Indiana*, in 1899, and its title might well have described its author, a proud Hoosier who wanted above all to be a commercial artist, or, failing that, a novelist, perhaps a playwright. A small bequest from his uncle Newton Booth, former Governor of California, had made it possible for him to spend the last years of the century in a leisurely apprenticeship in his hometown. He was in no hurry to go anywhere.

But in less than a year after his marriage to Louisa Fletcher and his election to the Indiana legislature he was stricken with so severe a case of typhoid fever that the family feared for his life. According to James Woodress, his biographer, Tarkington took his doctor's advice: to "recuperate in the healthiest place in the United States." The pines and the sea around Kennebunkport won him totally. When he left at the end of the summer, promising to return, he took his wife and his parents to Europe for a year of travel and rest. The year stretched into nine, and he did not resettle in Indianapolis until 1912 when he brought his second wife, Susanah Robinson, to occupy the old family home on Pennsylvania Avenue. The interim was spent in brief visits to England, Germany, and north Italian cities, prolonged stays in Florence and Capri, and what almost became permanent residence in Paris, Rome, and New York. Tarkington may have begun as a gentleman of leisure, an innocent abroad, but in less than a decade he was a successful novelist and playwright, a prolific short-story writer, and a wildly enthusiastic art collector. His avocation led, in time, to the letters in this collection.

Although this is hardly the occasion to rehearse Tarkington's long career, it is important to understand why Maine meant so much to this native of Indiana. We know that in the summer of 1910 he wanted to avoid the heat of New York City, and so he returned to Kennebunkport, unfortunately in the midst of marital troubles. After his divorce and remarriage, he and Susanah must have made summer visits to the East since we hear of his seeing in Maine, in 1914, another Indiana author, George Barr McCutcheon, and the following summer having a memorable lunch in York Harbor with William Dean Howells and Thomas Sergeant Perry. In 1916 he bought eighteen acres of land in Kennebunkport. A year later he enlarged the property and built a stately seven-bedroom house he called "Seawood." It faced the Kennebunk River on the west, deep woods and open fields on the east, and within a few years became the Tarkingtons' summer haven. They could live here as quietly as they wished, in comfortable retreat from their busy social life in Indianapolis. A luxury it obviously was, but Tarkington was almost fifty when he built "Seawood" and money, he always said, was made to be spent. He had made money.

George Horace Lorimer's *Saturday Evening Post* accepted *His Own People* for serialization after *Harper's Weekly* turned it down in 1906, and Tarkington thus became a regular contributor during the next four decades. In 1913, *Cosmopolitan* outbid *Everybody's Weekly* to publish the Penrod stories at prices that almost embarrassed the author. In the same year, F. N. Doubleday accepted *The Flirt*, an early Indianapolis novel, the first of thirty titles his company was happy to publish. And for years the theatre provided Tarkington with a steady income as well as the kind of challenge he thrived on. In 1901, he dramatized his own novel *Monsieur Beaucaire* for Richard Mansfield. In collaboration with Harry Leon Wilson, he wrote *The Man from Home* while living in Paris in the fall of 1906. George Tyler had it in production in New York ten months later and it ran for five years. Otis Skinner commissioned a play in 1909; Wilson and Tarkington delivered *Your Humble Servant* and Skinner played it for more than eighteen months. Between 1915 and 1931, Tarkington could not stay out of the theatre, in spite of the fact that he was producing his best fiction at the same time. He wrote *Clarence* in 1919 for the young Alfred Lunt and had the good fortune to cast the even younger Helen Hayes in the role of Cora Wheeler. Billie Burke opened in *Rose Briar* in 1922, Ruth Gordon in *Tweedles* the next season. And with the arrival of motion pictures and radio serials, Tarkington had even newer media to experiment with. Yet he knew they were not his serious work.

Tarkington was intent on earning his place in American letters through two vastly different kinds of fiction. *Penrod* (1914) and *Seventeen* (1916), the immensely popular novels of Midwestern youth and adolescence, were written out of boundless admiration for the "uncivilized" American boy and fond memories of the perils of growing up. His portraits of Penrod Schofield and Willie Baxter were modeled on his Indianapolis nephews and on the memories of his own boyhood. The four family chronicles—the early attack on business, *The Turmoil* (1914), the two Pulitzer prize novels, *The Magnificent Ambersons* (1918) and *Alice Adams* (1921), and the bleakest story of them all, *The Midlander* (1924)—are sharp social criticism of America's sudden transition from an agrarian to an industrial culture. If, compared to the fiction of Willa Cather and Edith Wharton, they now seem less acute than when they first appeared, that is not to discount the impact they had on the American people. Tarkington knew his métier and his audience. Throughout the Depression years he continued to write for that special audience with unabated success. When his eyesight began to fail in 1929 (he was totally blind for a period of five months), he learned to dictate to a secretary. *Mirthful Haven* (1930) was followed by *Mary's Neck* (1932) and *Presenting Lily Mars* (1933). His biographer believes that "Tarkington found himself at the peak of his grass-roots popularity . . . but scorned by many critics" chiefly because he was "a conservative in an age of social revolution." Whatever the reasons, he never permitted the literary journals to dictate his fictional methods any more than he allowed the New Deal to influence his politics. He was unashamedly traditionalist, Midwestern Republican · traditionalist, and he was overtly unhappy with the Roosevelt administration.

All the more understandable, then, was his instant infatuation in 1938 with two German-born classically-trained art historians, Erwin and Dora Panofsky. They had come to Kennebunkport as guests of three of their Princeton neighbors who shared houses in Maine and New Jersey, the English novelist I.A.R. Wylie and the medical doctors Louise Pearce and Josephine Baker. They had asked another summer resident, Madeleine Burrage, to meet the Panofskys one night at dinner, so the story goes. Miss Burrage told her sister Mildred, a painter, how impressed she was with the witty conversation of these Princeton visitors, and suggested introducing the newcomers to the Tarkingtons. The suggestion was typical Burrage generosity and, in this instance, perfectly timed. Tarkington was in the midst of writing *Some Old Portraits*, essays on twenty-two paintings in his collection, ranging from Paulus van Somer to Sir Thomas Lawrence. Although he was almost seventy, he was still an inquisitive student of art, self-trained but inherently perceptive. The forty-six-year-old Panofsky was completing his *Studies in Iconology: Humanistic Themes in the Art of the Renaissance.* He had earned his Ph.D. in art history at the University of Freiburg in 1914 and was one of the world's incomparable teachers. They did not remain strangers very long.

At the edge of his property, on the Kennebunk River, was a boat-house Tarkington called "The Floats." He and his neighbor, William Trotter, had turned it into a kind of private club, a gathering place for coffee and conversation, especially after a few hours at sea in the Tarkington motorboat. Panofsky was immediately a welcome "member," and for good reasons. John Coolidge, former director of Harvard's Fogg Art Museum, once compared living in Panofsky's ambience to "living next door to a lighthouse. Objectively you watched the beam revolve until suddenly you yourself were drenched by his ebullience, by his crackling perceptions, by his overwhelming, unaccountable kindness." During the next eight years, Tarkington and his friends discovered this ebullience for themselves as they came to know this remarkable man during his summer visits to Maine. He and his wife were eager to escape Princeton's humidity in July and August, reason enough for fleeing to the Maine coast, but something more must have caused them to return all through the war years to this quiet village. One would like to think it was the warmth with which they were received by the Trotters, the Grandemans, the Burrages, the Robertses—friends of Booth and Susanah Tarkington who appear and reappear in these letters— but it must also have been the contagious enthusiasm the Panofskys generated almost without knowing it and, very likely, the awe with which the elderly Tarkington listened to this learned yet modest European historian. Although his majestic works were yet to be written— *Albrecht Dürer* (1943), *Early Netherlandish Painting*

(1953), *Renaissance and Renascence* (1960)—he radiated
authority. His encyclopedic memory, his store of anecdotes, above all his quick wit and sharp tongue endeared him to generations of students. It is no surprise that he wrote to one of his old students in September, 1945, to say "We had a very delightful summer in good old Kennebunkport, where life begins at seventy and where we were treated extremely well." He had, without knowing it, said goodbye to Tarkington for the last time although they were still corresponding in late February, 1946, just three months before the novelist died. How had this unlikely friendship begun and why had it flourished? Panofsky's definition of a humanist—one who rejects authority but respects tradition—is partial explanation. They came from markedly different cultures but as humanists they shared a belief in independent judgments leisurely arrived at.

Born in Hannover, educated in Berlin and Freiburg, Panofsky had expected, like Tarkington, to spend his youth as a *Privatgelehrter* since he enjoyed a family inheritance and was in no hurry to teach or even to publish his doctoral dissertation on Albrecht Dürer. But post-war inflation abruptly changed his plans, and he accepted a post at the new University of Hamburg in 1921, first as *Privatdozent* and then as Professor. William Heckscher, one of his students in Hamburg, writes that "in the unquestionably glorious years of the Weimar Republic, Erwin Panofsky laid the foundation of his fame as a scholar who helped to change the aesthetic and antiquarian orientation of art history and turn it into a humanistic discipline. . . ." That fame, by 1931, was international, and New York University invited Panofsky as a visiting professor to its new graduate department of art history. He was here when he received notice, two years later, of his dismissal from the Hamburg faculty following the Nazi purge of the universities. With amazing adaptability (he knew English well, fortunately), he continued to teach in New York, then at Princeton University, and finally accepted Abraham Flexner's invitation to join his newly founded Institute for Advanced Study in Princeton as one of the first permanent members of its School of Humanistic Studies. From this prestigious institution Panofsky and his wife were vacationing when they met the Tarkingtons in 1938.

What sealed their friendship was not only a mutual devotion to painting but a zest for life, for new experience. The correspondence between the two men, as we read it now, can only delight us with its catholicity. Their letters touch on art and literature, international politics, anti-Semitism, the New Deal, Nobel prize winners, book reviewers, dogs, gallery owners, Indiana Republicans, Yale University, taxi drivers, air raid wardens, the military mind, Kennebunkport natives, family illness, and, as World War II progressed, the atom bomb and the chances for man's survival. Generosity of spirit is in every page. The originals of these letters also reveal a pleasantly old-fashioned quality that is missing, alas, from much of our world. Tarkington may have dictated his novels but not his letters to his Princeton friends. In spite of failing eyesight, he answered Panofsky's handwritten letters with a shaky but determined pen. And from the first letter to the last, the salutations never varied: Dear Dr. Panofsky, Dear Mr. Tarkingon. *Dulce et decorum est.*

It is a pleasure to acknowledge here my debts in editing this correspondence. Mrs. Gerda Panofsky not only granted permission to publish her husband's letters but also provided me with much good advice and innumerable facts for the headnotes. Richard Cary, Curator of Rare Books and Manuscripts, Colby College Library, graciously supplied me with copies of twenty-two Panofsky letters in their Tarkington collection and for the purpose of photographic reproduction allowed me to use the original of one of them. The Merchants National Bank and Trust Company of Indianapolis, Agent for the Tarkington Literary Properties, has granted permission to publish the Tarkington letters. James Woodress' *Booth Tarkington: Gentleman from Indiana* (Philadelphia, 1955) was an invaluable source of information as was William S. Heckscher's "Erwin Panofsky: A Curriculum Vitae" (*Record of the Art Museum, Princeton University*, XXVII, 1969).

To friends of the correspondents I owe thanks for their reminiscences and their patient answering of my questions: David and Nancy Coffin, Emma Greene Epps, Marian Grandeman, Elizabeth Trotter, and especially Mildred and Madeleine Burrage. To Princeton friends and colleagues, I am indebted for a variety of reasons: Samuel D. Atkins, G. E. Bentley, Mary Bertagni, Mina R. Bryan, Beatrice Earle, J. Arthur Hanson, Martha Lou Stohlman, Robert H. Taylor, Willard Thorp, and the Staff of the Rare Book Room, Princeton University Library.

April, 1974   Richard M. Ludwig
Princeton, New Jersey

Dr Panofsky
& Mr Tarkington

The summer of 1938 was particularly memorable in the Tarkington household in Kennebunkport. The visitors from Princeton were soon introduced to the ritual of afternoon tea at "The Floats" and on occasion buffet supper parties followed by music and good conversation over coffee. Tarkington had been collecting paintings since 1903 (Gainsboroughs, Stuarts, Romneys, Raeburns, as well as a Titian, a Goya, and a Velasquez), so he must have been an avid listener to Erwin Panofsky's encyclopedic lore. The article on the Florentine painter, Piero di Cosimo, appeared in The Worcester Art Museum Annual, II (1937-1938), 32ff.

Elizabeth Trotter, daughter of William Trotter, co-owner of "The Floats," became Tarkington's secretary in 1929 when blindness threatened him and he had to learn to dictate his novels. The Trotters spent winters in Chestnut Hill, Philadelphia, and summers in Kennebunkport; but in a short time Betty became a member of the Tarkington family, traveling with them to Indianapolis in October or November and back to "Seawood" in the spring. She appears with increasing frequency in these letters since she was carrying on, during the war years, her own correspondence with the Panofskys.

Dr Panofsky
& Mr Tarkington

114 Prospect Ave.
Princeton, N. J.
July 30th, 1938

Dear Mr. Tarkington,

You and Mrs. Tarkington have been so unbelievably kind to us that I wish to express our gratitude by a symbol, however poor. I am sending you, with some misgivings, that little article on two pictures by Piero di Cosimo of whom you are as fond as I am. It is a pity that I have nothing else to offer you; I hope that a book on Renaissance iconography, which will appear within a few months, will make a more adequate token of gratitude—at least as far as volume is concerned.

It has been a great privilege to enjoy the hospitality of your home and the charm of your boat-house, and to talk to a great writer who is also an art lover and a philosopher in his own right. But, setting aside all this, it was a wonderful experience to meet a homo liberalis atque humanus. In this respect your kindness and sympathy has meant more to us than I can say.

With our renewed thanks, and our very best wishes for yourself, Mrs. Tarkington and all your friends, especially Miss Trotter,

Most sincerely yours,
Erwin Panofsky

The "old book" Tarkington sent to Princeton was Mirthful Haven *(1930), ironically titled since it was an angry denunciation of the way*

certain "summer people" behaved toward the Kennebunkport "natives." His portrait of Captain Embury in this novel is drawn from a long acquaintance with one of the last of the authentic deep-sea captains, Dan Dudley, who owned an old antiques-filled house near Ocean Avenue. He used to entertain Tarkington and his summer visitors with stories about clipper ships and local customs.

Seawood
Kennebunkport, Maine
August 5, 1938

Dear Mr. Panofsky:—

It was delightful to have your indulgent letter, which stimulated an ever-ready vanity; but no-no-no! the debt was all *ours* and Kennebunkport's. You and your brilliant and genial family illuminated the summer for us, and the best to be said for us is that all of us understand what a privilege was ours while you were here.

Thank you indeed for The Worcester Museum Annual containing your asborbing Piero di Cosimo article and the interesting notes thereon. *What* a man he was and how quietly you have been able to master and contain him! Then—unobtrusively, and I'd almost say, slyly—you give him to us. (I mean that you hardly let us suspect we're recipients of the gift.)

I shall presently send you an old book of mine upon an aspect of this place about which you've felt some bitterness, I fear—a relation between the "Natives" and one type of "summer people." However, there's a fairly true portrait of Cap'n Dan Dudley, who sleeps now among his ancestors and other seafarers.

Miss Burrage came last night for something that might be called a Panofsky party, in reminiscence.

We all of us send our very best remembrance and feel
that injustice will be done us if all of you do not
return next year.

Gratefully yours,
Booth Tarkington

In August, 1938, the Panofskys moved to 97 Bat-
tle Road, a white frame house on the edge of the
Institute for Advanced Study grounds and their
Princeton residence for the rest of their lives.
Both of their sons were graduated from the Uni-
versity in the Class of 1938, Wolfgang (as saluta-
torian) at the age of nineteen and Hans at the age
of twenty.

114 Prospect Ave.
Princeton, N. J.
August 16th, 1938

Dear Mr. Tarkington,

I did not want to thank you for the kind and generous
gift of your "Mirthful Haven" before having read it.
Now, to say that I have done so would be a very
inadequate description. Your book has a strangely
compelling power, not unlike the undertow in the
water, which makes the process of "reading" not a
matter of willful and detached assimilation, but of
complete and, as it were, semi-hypnotic obedience.
The tension, or suspense, it seemed to me, is of an
entirely inward character; the reader asks himself, not:
"what is going to happen to the characters?" but:
"what is going to happen to me?" That we know Kennebunkport—however superficially—and even the
picture of "Captain Embury" which you were kind
enough to show us was, of course, an additional
stimulus. But even without that, I should say, the

6 book could have enthralled me as an unparalleled presentation of the interconnection between people and places, and between the present and an inescapable past.

It was a little hard at first to reconcile oneself with the hot dampness and utter desertedness of a Princeton August after a Kennebunkport July. But it had to be done, and there is even a peculiar, unreal charm about the place. There are also certain things such as straightening out one's photographs and galley-proof reading which can only be done with the mind in low gear, so to speak. My older son has already reached his destination in California, and the other is going to leave us by the end of the month. But in between we shall move into our new little house, where [we] shall settle down to a quiet old age ("as a decrepit father takes delight to see his active child do deeds of youth"), and where your book will occupy the place of honour in my study.

With my renewed thanks (also for your kind and truly encouraging words about my little Piero article) and respectful greetings, "von Haus zu Haus" as the German expression is,

yours most sincerely,
Erwin Panofsky

Panofsky's Studies in Iconology: Humanistic Themes in the Art of the Renaissance *was first published by Oxford University Press in 1939. It is in no sense a "little" book. Based on six Mary Flexner Lectures given at Bryn Mawr College, it illustrates Panofsky's definition of iconography ("that branch of the history of art which concerns itself with the subject matter or meaning of works of art, as opposed to their form") through almost one hundred plates and a close analysis of certain works by Piero di Cosimo and Michelangelo, of the "pseudomorphosis" during the Renaissance of two reputedly classical figures, Father Time and Blind Cupid, and of the Florentine Neoplatonists, particularly Marsilio Ficino.*

David Silberman and his younger brother Abris were New York art dealers who visited the Tarkingtons in both Indiana and in Maine. Nellie Eldredge was for many years the maid of one of their Kennebunkport neighbors, Miss Sarah Bancroft.

Seawood
Kennebunkport, Maine
Sept. 5, 1939

Dear Mr. Panofsky:

Your "little book" (your astounding description!) arrived today, bearing an inscription that fairly shames us, so conscious we are that we do not merit it. I have just finished the Introduction which, of itself, is an exposition to keep one thinking long and long—and, for my poor part, must be read again with the concentration necessary for following thinking so close.

The rest of the book stretches out before this reader fascinatingly—delectable vast fields in which one is to walk if one worthily can. I should say at once that your mastery of expression dumbfounds us again—it has often done so—and the "printed word" proves itself always to be your own because it carries the sound of your very voice.

We have missed the Panofskys severely; they seem now to have been here but a moment—one that we failed to squeeze to its utmost. Their departure left a tameness in the air. Mr. David Silberman did his best to enliven and console us; and I must say that in "The Game" at the "Floats" on Sunday evening he drove

8 all other thoughts from our minds for some hilarious minutes. With convincing clarity he enacted three words: "customer," "steals," and "her." Then an inspired Garrick Player made a guess miraculously correct: "Nor custom stale her infinite variety."

Already Labor Day has taken the "summer people" look from the village. The Native returns to his own. One, a semi-Native, called on me, for which I owe you another pleasure. This was Nellie's niece, young Mary, who left us all marveling, yet she is only of *her* American generation. She has poise and voice and enunciation enough for the stage—looks and manner, too, of course. I couldn't suggest much that would be of use to her, I fear.

I think the "Seventeen" episode was so ephemeral that it died next day, as it were. Not even a vaporous repercussion was heard—nothing. And now the village, the Old Road and the River Road, begin their autumnal doze; the young plod soberly to school and in the noon hour talk of war—war far away!

When you left I did not think it would come. Some profound force has produced it—produced Hitler and all the germs that probably keep the balance-of-things that allows us to move toward real civilization along a dipping but eventually ascending spiral road.

How lovely to turn to your great book—I *see* it is that—away from the heaving blackened present hour!

Gratefully and gratefully,
Booth Tarkington

Being the kind of novelist he was, Tarkington exulted in Kennebunkport's "natives" and their peculiar quirks, their knowledge of local history, and their stoic endurance of the "summer people." Francis Noble was a laconic, moody ex-newspaperman, a "gentleman drinker" who lived a hermit's life in a small shack across the river from "The Floats" but turned up almost every afternoon for tea. Some of his friends called him "Cozy," but not Booth Tarkington. Eddie Wells was a feeble-minded man with a wooden leg who spent most of his time in the village square, near Weinstein's grocery store. Unable to talk, he was nevertheless the first to know the town's gossip, or so it was said.

The "horrible book" by Hermann Rauschning was either Hitler Speaks: A Series of Political Conversations with Adolf Hitler on His Real Aims *or* Germany's Revolution of Destruction, *two exposés published in London in 1939.*

Seawood
Kennebunkport, Maine
Oct. 15, '39

Dear Mr. Panofsky:—

It's almost a week since Mrs. Tarkington finished the reading of your great book aloud to me; this seems my first opportunity to express a little of my gratitude and a like small amount of the amazement that fills us both. Our feeling is that you well might look up to yourself with a peculiar awe—one might almost say alarm! Certainly that is our view of you.

There is a charm in the book that comes so natively from you that you may be unaware of it. This: that although your reader may continually be conscious of his little learning, and thus take shame of a misspent youth, he always feels that you overlook it and deal gently with him, courteously treating him as if he already knew much of what you tell him—which he doesn't.

Probably (I'd say certainly) the two figures now become *most* memorably comprehended under *your* tutelage: Piero di Cosimo and Michelangelo. I think I [had] no more than [a] glimpse of a bit of them before, especially the latter. Your interpretations are light itself. How grateful those two should be! . . .

The village is wrapped in its autumnal silence now; the horn of the hunter is heard in the woods (if a shotgun may be so poetized) and only the *real* fishing boats brave the icy breezes outside the little harbor mouth. At "The Floats" we sit heavily rugged, watch the gulls prod for clams, and listen to their salty cater-waulings. There's ice on the ponds in the morning; Mr. Noble and Eddie Wells have frosty noses and Dock Square is empty all day long. Except for the gaunt hotels and bleakly shuttered cottages, there's nothing left but the old beginnings of things—the little Yankee fishing village itself. Yet we linger on the skirts of it—year after year after year, and would not willingly be elsewhere.

We try to hear the news—the dreadful news—as if it weren't of today and as if it were "only history"; but after reading that horrible book by Rauschning and feeling the infernal truth in it, we find it difficult not to realize that the nightmares are contemporaneous. I hope that they don't press heavily upon you or upon Mrs. Panofsky. Also that you and she and your sons are in excellent health.

All of this household wish to be remembered to you and to Mrs. Panofsky; they ask me to urge Kennebunkport upon you for next summer with vehement eloquence; but I can do it only with the vehemence.

Again—and again—gratefully

Yours,
Booth Tarkington

Dear Mr. Tarkington,

If there is one thing which dims the sheer delight of having been admitted to the circle of your admiring friends it is the feeling of being always in your debt. I had hoped to have reciprocated, however modestly, some of your kindness and generosity by sending you my book, and now you have repaid this small gift seventy times seven by writing me, with your own hand, two letters which make me proud with joy and red with shame, and which will always be kept among my most cherished possessions. Please accept my humble thanks for your kind words. They have been a very great comfort to me quite apart from their personal value. It is very hard to express oneself in a foreign tongue, and he who has some feeling for the richness and innate beauty of the English language is particularly conscious of his shortcomings. Many of my friends have told me that my English, though perhaps not downright faulty from a grammatical point of view, was much too pedantic and, at the same time, too obtrusively personal to pass muster with the critics, and I know very well that their objections are justified in many respects. Yet I could never bring myself to writing my things in German and to having them translated by others—a procedure which is comparable to the ruinous habit of most modern sculptors of merely modelling their statues in clay while leaving the execution in marble to a "technician." You can imagine what it meant to me that you, a great master of the English language, had such kind words just for the style of my little book. You have generously overlooked a lack of skill which others have not failed to notice and, finally, preferred the somewhat uneven texture of a sculpture directly carved from the stone to the smooth perfection which a professional "translator" might have attained. I am deeply grateful for this encouragement, and also for what you say about my interpretative endeavors as such. Only, what I have tried to make clear is really not entirely original. It is perhaps only in contrast with so many purely formalistic interpretations of works of art that iconographic efforts appear as something unusual. In reality, my methods are reactionary rather than revolutionary, and I should not be surprised if some critics would tell me what the old doctor in "Doctor's Dilemma" tells his young friend: "You can be proud that your discovery has last been made forty years ago," or something to that effect. In this matter, too, I am delighted to find myself in agreement with you. Your wonderful remark about the "courtesy" which we owe to the old masters in at least trying to listen to what they wished to tell us sums up all anyone could say about the aims of the history of art.

We are both happy to hear that you and Mrs. Tarkington have spent the rest of the summer in good health and spirits and still enjoy the autumnal beauty of Kennebunkport which must indeed be marvellous to behold. For us, the atmosphere of your boat-house is both a memory and a hope—a condensed realization of all that which ought to survive and perhaps will survive in spite of everything.

With our warmest wishes for you and your whole happy family, particularly Mrs. Tarkington and Miss Trotter,

I am devotedly and gratefully yours,
Erwin Panofsky

July 27, 1940

Dear Mr. Tarkington,

We are very much afraid that you must look upon
us as traitors to the community of Kennebunkport
and to the State of Maine. Yet we do hope you will
allow us to offer our wishes for the next year of your
life. We have "found" (to quote from "Mary's Neck")
an object which may amuse you: the walking stick of
Captain Crowell who was quite a character on Cape
Cod. Probably you will not have much use for it
(though the ivory knob is nice to the touch), but it may
do as another item in your collection of maritime odds
and ends.

If it were not for the nostalgic remembrance of
our good friends, the Burrages, and, above all, of the
unforgettable hours on the Floats, on your motor boat
and in your house we should be very happy here,—not
in spite but because of the general state of the world
which fills us with gratitude for every new day of life
in a great and wonderful country. Cape Cod is so
different from Kennebunkport that one can love both
without forsaking either. The contrast between the two
brings to mind the good old antithesis between the
Beautiful and the Sublime. The Cape is simpler, less
picturesque, less rich in the sheer loveliness of ancient
trees and lordly houses, but it is very grandiose, with
miles and miles of unbroken sands, rolling dunes and
hundreds of deserted circular freshwater ponds in
the midst of almost pathless woods. . . .

In spite of all these advantages we wish that we were
able to greet you personally on your birthday. Let us
hope that we may do so in 1941, and that the year
which begins day-after-tomorrow may be a happy one
for you and yours, so that you may continue to give

14 joy and hope to all those who admire you as a writer and revere you as a man.

With our best wishes, also for Mrs. Tarkington and the Trotter ladies,

devotedly yours,
Dora and Erwin Panofsky

The Panofskys were obviously missed in Kennebunkport during the summer of 1940, but Tarkington was not entirely without conversations about painting. Dr. Hans Tietze and his wife Erica Tietze-Conrat were both prominent art historians. Their double portrait, painted by Oskar Kokoschka in 1909, is now in the Museum of Modern Art, New York.

Mildred and Madeleine Burrage were often visitors at the Tarkington house, having moved to Kennebunkport in 1918, the year after "Seawood" was built. They owned an 1807 sea-captain's house, "Homeport," where Mildred painted and Madeleine (called "Bob" by her family) designed and made gold and silver jewelry. Tarkington used to astound his family with his enormous reserves of energy. The Burrages astounded Tarkington.

The "Zan Tee" was a forty-five foot motorboat named for Susanah Tarkington, the novelist's wife, and skippered by Harry Thirkell. During the summer and fall, Tarkington and his guests regularly enjoyed afternoons at sea, followed by hot tea and coffee at "The Floats."

Kennebunkport, Maine
August 1, '40
Dear Dr. and Mrs. Panofsky:

In our hallway, as you come in, you see the implica-
tion of the visitor who has just preceded you; and
you know that in a moment you will meet him. Moreover, you have quite an idea of his dress, of his quality,
and of the dignity that he maintains; and, as he is of
these shores, you are sure that he is a seafarer of
consequence—Master of a ship, no less. Who else would
bring home the hybrid rod, topped with ivory of so
agreeable a shape?

The Captain, in brief, has left his cane there,
under the engraving of Sir Joshua Reynolds, and he
must be now in the living-room, carrying his top-hat
and gloves with him, in high stateliness, as he talks of
Chinese Seas, Sumatra, Callao, and Bombay curries,
and nibbles cake and tosses down his glass of wine.

Never *was* there a more eloquent cane, and we
don't see how you could bring yourselves to give it
up. My debt is great, too, for the letter, for your remem-
bering that I was having another birthday. Such
kindness helps one to be calm under the indignity of
enlarging numbers.

How we have missed you all and have inveighed
against Cape Cod! With the Burrages we begin all
conversations by speaking of this loss, and we have
sprung a leak intellectually. What little we knew of
Art has run into dry sands; and though Dr. and Mrs.
Tietze and their son and daughter-in-law stopped for
an afternoon and evening, the hole was not plugged.
Nor are we consoled by knowing how pleased you are
to have your older son with you and "the little one"
performing miracles in the West. Happiness on Cape
Cod may mean a return to it another year—though,

16 naturally, we are respectable enough to wish you to be entirely happy, wherever you are.

Next year, however, must see Mrs. Panofsky on the high rock waving to the "Zan Tee" as it comes home to the river bringing her husband safely to supper at "The Floats."

All of us send our best wishes and I am

Yours indeed gratefully again,
Booth Tarkington

The Fighting Littles (1941) is not one of Tarkington's better novels; in fact it is not much more than a series of stories focused on one family in a midwestern city. The father, Ripley Little, so violently attacks the New Deal that he becomes almost a caricature Republican, but he also served during the writing of this book as "an emotional outlet for the author," as Tarkington's biographer so wisely describes him. "It's a most helpful device," he wrote to his friend Hugh Kahler. "If I 'make' the image screech, my voice need but murmur." Into Ripley Little went much of Tarkington's outrage at Franklin Roosevelt's abuse of authority.

Albrecht Dürer, on the other hand, is Panofsky's magnum opus, but it did not appear until 1943. It is a recurring subject in the letters to come.

Princeton, N. J.
97 Battle Road
December 27, 1941

Dear Mr. and Mrs. Tarkington, dear Miss Trotter,

We are both overjoyed and embarrassed by the precious gift of the "Fighting Littles"—which I have

not yet read because my wife took it away from me
at once and strictly refuses to let go of it, being entirely
fascinated. We are overjoyed because it is a new token
of a friendship which we value above most other things
in life, and embarrassed because I have nothing to
offer in return. I had hoped to present to you, again,
the first copy of a new "opus"—a rather comprehensive
monograph on Dürer which sums up an almost life-
long occupation with this gentleman—, but although
the Princeton Press is prepared to risk a small fortune,
and although the Council of Learned Societies very
handsomely granted a subsidy for publication, there
is still a gap or chasm of $1250 which separates the
intention from the accomplishment, and I am fully
aware of the fact that, in this day and age, quite a few
things are more important than a book on Dürer.
Thus I have put away my manuscript for the benefit
of a future historian of the history of art—but the sad
thing about it is that I had also to bury my hope of
giving it to you as a Christmas present; we have nothing
to offer except our warmest wishes for a New Year
which will hardly be a happy but may and, let us
hope, will be a brave and victorious one. Perhaps your
next birthday, dear Mr. Tarkington, will already be
celebrated in an atmosphere of ultimate assurance, and
this time we hope to be among your admirers and
well-wishers; for nothing will induce me to venture
into the mountains again.

In the meantime we wish and pray for your health
and happiness. With our renewed thanks,

> yours as ever devotedly,
> Dora and Erwin Panofsky

*This letter is written on an oversize sheet of
orange cardboard that may have been print-shop
surplus, in days of paper shortage, but it was also*

a color which eased Tarkington's failing eye-sight. He used many more such sheets for making notes for his next two novels.

The annual hegira from "Seawood," Kenne-bunkport, to 4270 North Meridian Street, Indianapolis, always included a stopover at the Trotters' Chestnut Hill estate, called Cleeve Gate, on the edge of the Wissahickon. The Panofskys either visited at the same time or invited the Tarkingtons to drive over to Princeton for their autumn reunion.

[Kennebunkport]

Dear Mr. Panofsky: Oct. 17, '42

I hope that "global war" excuses any kind of "stationery," including this!

We are more disappointed than you'd know, and Urbana has proved its indifference to us and to that old art now popularly known (as if it were something new) as "timing." We are always fastened down at Kenne-bunkport until either just before Christmas or just before Thanksgiving. Our only hope of seeing you and Mrs. Panofsky rests in the proximity of Princeton to Chestnut Hill. This year we expect to arrive at Mrs. Trotter's a day or two before Thanksgiving; and we shall try to arrange for a vocal account of the Illinois excursion.

It is a personal deprivation not to be in Indianapolis and to receive what would be almost certainly a guarded modicum of your impressions of that city's appearance to a traveler. (Not that I doubt your finding enough that's good in our midland country.)

Again we missed you here, and sometimes, as the "Zan Tee" (now conspicuously the I. F. I.) curves to slide into the river, we see the figure of a lady waving a hand from the crest of the coastal rocks where she watched for you. This year you'd have been an "Observer." (We are permitted to carry "Observers.") None sail with us now for our final chilly patrols of '42 and we "retire from the service" November first, having been "as safe as a church" the whole season apparently, and having seen no trace of the enemy except one great surge of oil we think *had* been his.

Kennebunkport in war time would have interested you: the village turns up some queer facets to the light—as Betty discovered after she took charge of "The Point" as Head Air Warden. She accomplished a perfect dimout, however. Of course the "natives" had to rise superior to their natures and submit to a bad financial season. It couldn't be *wholly* concealed from the summer visitors that *some*body was causing explosions in this general neighborhood—especially when hotels and cottages shook upon their foundations!

The Burrages, I need not be telling you, are, and have been, in incessant motion. War has only made it more rapid, vigorous, and eloquent. You and Mrs. Panofsky will easily imagine Mildred's activity when our Patriot Scrap Heap suffered from pilferings.

Our best to all of your family including the addition we hope you find both wise and charming—and we look forward to the possibilities of Chestnut Hill in November.

> Faithfully yours,
> Booth Tarkington

> *Among the many things Tarkington and Panofsky had in common was their love for dogs. In fact in 1945 Panofsky even dreamt his own epitaph, so he told one of his former pupils, Harry Bober:*
>> *He hated babies, gardening, and birds;*
>> *But loved a few adults, all dogs, and words.*

*The big dog he loaned to the K-9 Corps was easy
to love, a black French Briard named Cyrano
when he arrived on Battle Road but soon called
Moses by his master. After a year of trying to train
him, the Army sent Moses back, discharged for
homesickness.*

*Emma Greene joined the Panfosky household
as a cook in 1934, shortly after they settled in
Princeton, and worked for the family until
Panofsky died in 1968. She made only one visit
with them to Kennebunkport.*

97 Battle Road
Princeton, N. J.
October 20, 1942

Dear Mr. Tarkington,

Of course, it will be sad to pass through Indianapolis without greeting you (I don't know whether there
is an English equivalent of the German phrase "to be
in Rome without seeing the Pope"); but your kind
letter is an ample compensation—not only in that it
assures us of your absolution from the sin of faithlessness
toward Kennebunkport but also, or even more so,
in that it bears witness to your good health and spirits.
In comparison with your and Betty Trotter's exploits
—not to mention the Burrages—our own contribution
to the "war effort" looks more than insignificant. We
are both, since Pearl Harbor, assiduous airplane spot-
ters, proud of having contributed by our very con-
scientiousness, to a number of false alarms in New York
City; I have been promoted, after much practice, to
Second Assistant Nozzle-Holder in the Decontamination
Squad, a tough outfit which is supposed to clean up
after air raids or gas attacks (it is quite an experience
to hold on to a fire hose when a feeble-minded member

of the English Department turns on the water full blast); and I have handed over my big dog to a Sergeant whom he helps to guard a military objective, attacking every comer on sight. I wish we could do more, and we will if and when required.

To see you all in November would give us the greatest pleasure imaginable, especially if you could manage to have a meal in our little house in Princeton. It is not much of a house, but we have still our fairly competent cook. But if this should be too much of a bother for you we shall be delighted to meet you, even for only five minutes, wherever you say.

With all our best wishes,
Devotedly yours
Erwin Panofsky

Would you be kind enough to give our love to the Burrages when you see them?

In the summer of 1943, during their two-month escape from the Princeton humidity, the Panofskys lived in "Tory Chimneys," a house built in the late eighteenth century by a sailmaker from Marblehead and owned by the Burrage family. On July 29, the Tarkingtons celebrated Booth's birthday with their usual large dinner party for old friends, and the Panofskys composed a little poem to accompany their gift.

97 Battle Road
Princeton, N. J.
June 2, 1943

Dear Mr. Tarkington,

How kind of you to write us such a long and friendly letter, and this in the throes of a recent arrival! We refuse to be persuaded that a gift is not a gift, but your and the Burrages' attempt to do so makes it all the easier for us to accept it. With such good friends as the Burrages are we have no hesitation whatsoever, and your letter is quite enough to eliminate the last vestiges of embarrassment. We have already written them to accept their gracious offer and shall appear in Kennebunkport on the first of July, barring what Shipping and Insurance Companies are fond of calling an "Act of God." So we look forward to the pleasures of a pastoral life and, first of all, to happy hours on The Floats.

In immense "Vorfreude" (a term only feebly rendered by "anticipation") and with our warmest wishes for yourself and all the members of your narrower and wider family,

Yours as ever devotedly,
Dora and Erwin Panofsky

Inscribèd be this glass to one
Who by his works and by his life
Spreads "happiness" instead of strife;
Who understands the grief of boys,
And ageing people's wistful joys,
And Tintoretto *père* and son;
Who loves Sir Joshua and whales,
Ben Jonson and old captains' tales;
Who knows the souls of men and dogs,
Midwestern plains and ocean fogs;
Who can converse with Gay and Donne;
Whose mind embraces centuries
While conning small-town tragedies;
Who looks upon the human race
With impish wit and God-like grace:
In other words, Booth Tarkington.

Dora and Erwin Panofsky
Kennebunkport, July 29, 1943

The two-volume Albrecht Dürer *was published by Princeton University Press in June, 1943, the first volume devoted to text and the second to a handlist of the works and 325 illustrations. With his usual modest understatement, Panofsky explains in the preface that this book "developed from the Norman Wait Harris lecture delivered at Northwestern University in 1938. It is therefore addressed to a 'mixed audience' rather than to scholars." But of course the book was "begun" long before he left Germany and grew, in several stages, into what H. W. Janson called "the finest monograph of its kind and a model of empathy as well as meticulous scholarship."*

The "little article" referred to, titled "Conrad Celtes and Kunz von der Rosen: Two Problems in Portrait Identification," appeared in The Art Bulletin, *XXIV (1942), 39 ff.*

97 Battle Road
Princeton, N. J.
September 23, 1943

Dear Mr. Tarkington,

Dora, who arrived yesterday night, told me that she left you well and in good spirits after the exertions of our farewell coffee party, and this was a great comfort to me. I was deeply touched, but at the same time a little disturbed by your kindness in coming to our house in spite of your headache, and it is a relief to know that you had not to suffer for this kindness afterwards.

My own journey was not so bad at all. It started in a Caravaggiesque *tenebroso* atmosphere on Kennebunk Station where enormous piles of luggage were arranged in picturesque disorder, waiting, allegedly, for three days to be removed. The baggage master was deeply offended when I voiced the desire to increase the pile by two more suitcases; but the irresistible force of a Dollar bill met the movable object of his mind, with the result—epoch-making in the history of American railroading—that the suitcases arrived in Princeton simultaneously with myself. On the train I got a bench by myself from Dover, and by changing from the position of an embryo to that of the Slave on the left of Michelangelo's Libyan Sibyl (and back) I slept quite well and was able to give my keenest attention to the question whether or not the big cherry tree in front of the Institute should be surrounded by a circular bench.

I am reporting these details only because you and Mrs. Tarkington were so full of kind concern and compassion about what the "Boston and Maine" would do to me. But the main reason for writing is, of course, to thank you again and again for all the kindness we received from you during this wonderful summer—ranging from cigarettes, and flowers, and vegetables, and books, and "the game" to those perfect hours on the Floats. I am quite serious in saying that I consider your friendship one of the greatest favors Fate has bestowed upon me. Meeting you is meeting a whole world (most of which was entirely new to me) and a whole period of history. This year, I have to be particularly thankful for the encouragement you gave me in relation to my Dürer book. In arranging it as I did I ventured the attempt to sit on two stools (with the probable result of sitting between them), namely, to be more or less readable and yet not altogether amateurish. Now, my critics will all be "professionals," and most of them will be German-born like myself. They will naturally and quite legitimately concentrate on factual errors (of which there will be many) and controversial problems of a specialized nature, and none of them will be willing (or able) to tell me to what extent I have succeeded in writing a book, so to speak; and this is precisely what no author can know by himself. So you can imagine what *your* approval meant to me. Of course, you looked upon my book with an especially benevolent eye; but even so I feel very much elated. My colleagues here tell me mostly how beautiful the printing is, and Yale has ordered a copy "on approval with the right to return it should it prove to be decidedly inferior"—upon which the Princeton Press has answered that they were not sure whether it was inferior, but that they hoped not decidedly so.

I am including two copies of a little article on portraiture in the graphic media, one for you (but not to read, only to admire the gentleman with the moustache), the other for Miss Trotter in return for the fishes.

With all good wishes from both of us and more thanks than can be expressed by mouth or pen,

Yours devotedly,
Erwin Panofsky

On November 18, 1899, William Dean Howells visited Indianapolis; and the young Tarkington, having just published his first novel, The Gentleman from Indiana, *was honored to be his guide around the city. Sometime during the day, Howells, then over sixty, gave the thirty-year-old Tarkington a warning about critics that he still remembered in 1943.*

Figaro, a large black poodle and reigning member of the Tarkington canine corps, had been preceded by Gamin, bought in France during a vacation abroad, and by Lorenzo the Magnificent, known as Wops. Tarkington's biographer recalls the novelist's saying that French

poodles "are made of black sunshine . . . the friendliest humorists in the world." Figaro's contemporaries were considerably smaller spaniels named Peter and Rennie.

[Kennebunkport]
Sept. 30-'43

Dear Dr. Panofsky:

Thank you for your letter, for The Art Bulletin, and for so many other things that "I don't know where to begin."

Seems to me you set a most helpful model for portrait identification. I interrupt my A[lbrecht] D[ürer] reading to study these intricacies and am rewarded in many manners, not the least of them being a further acquaintance with your favorite ghost—that of Willibald Pirckheimer. It was delightful to find him on the last of your pages as well as on the first. How genial a haunting!

I can't imagine anybody's doubting the "cases" you make for Celtes and von der Rosen—not even poor Mrs. Tietze! Something in the posture of Celtes with A. D. suggests a fancy that maybe the latter saw himself, pro tem, as a sort of Dante conducted by a valued courier who's knowingly point[ing] out the Sights.—However, I spoke of your paper as "helpful," and it is; but it's also a carrier of despair. How the devil is a head so empty of all save evanescences as mine to rely on itself for certainties about anything, let alone even probabilities about old works of art?

I hope that Yale will select Goeb[b]els for its next President, just to be consistent with its purchasing policy, and that your colleagues have recovered from their joy in A. D.'s outer garments. For a novelist such surface is usually the paper "jacket" of a book; during well nigh half a century friends of mine have found the "jackets" safe and saving. When I was a "young author" the best old one said to me of reviewers: "They can still hurt you—long after their capacity to please you has passed." Poor Tennyson compared the person who wrote—or spoke to him—of his work to a tiny figure almost invisible on the horizon; but it shot an arrow that came all the way and lodged in the poet's heart. On the other hand there are things like this. Mrs. Trotter has just disappointed us. Knowing that she had to save for heavy taxes, we planned to take A. D. to her as a Thanksgiving present; but she wrote Betty that she's purchased a copy, as of all the world this was the book she most wished to possess.

Mildred blew in yesterday. I deplore that phrase as bad slang; but with "the Burrages," as you know, it isn't slang at all. She blew into the "Floats" shouting that she'd been fired, and we greeted the good news warmly. Mr. Noble tried to look cryptic, and Figaro, though he had inside disagreements with recent meals, barked his special Burrage bark for no short time. Then we sat and talked of how woefully everybody misses all the Panofskys. That, however, was no new subject. You and Mrs. Panofsky have left your portraits —or, rather, your smiling effigies—in the wide old doorway with the dark shapes of ship models and figureheads vague in the background. So this wartime summer was a good, wise, happy one.

Gratefully yours,
Booth Tarkington

It is not difficult to guess why Tarkington chose these three novels to send to the Panofskys. Gentle Julia (1922), a kind of sequel to the popular Seventeen, *devotes two chapters to a comical poodle named Gamin. The Plutocrat (1927) contains a hero modeled on a Kennebunkport neigh-*

bor and traveling companion, Howard Fisher. The Lorenzo Bunch (1936) is a novel the author says he wrote "for more rarefied minds, those capable of detachment." Panofsky calls the conclusion of this last novel "one of the most moving things I have ever read." Strangely enough it is this same last chapter which McCall's *had bluntly rejected during serialization because of its subject matter: a sticky divorce and a doomed second marriage.*

Betty Trotter's translation of Léo Mouton's Le demi-roi: duc d'Épernon *appeared in 1935 under the title* Epernon of Old France. *It is a biography of Jean Louis de Nogaret de la Valette, the sixteenth-century courtier and politician, governor of Limousin under Henry IV.*

Panofsky's dog Moses had, by 1943, been replaced by a noble red setter named Jerry.

97 Battle Road
Princeton, N. J.
October 1, 1943

Dear Mr. Tarkington,

We did not want to thank you for the four books—what a magnificent present again!—before having read or re-read them; and this morning, when I sat down at my desk with pen in hand, in came the postman with another present—your letter. So it cannot be helped: we just have to reconcile ourselves to the idea that it is forever impossible not to be in your debt and can only try, like Mr. Noble when he plays the word "honesty," to search our vest pockets for mostly non-existent pennies.

Concerning the books, the trouble is that to read them requires a mind which works like those gas meters with three separate dials, the hand on the first

moving very fast, that on the second at a medium
speed, and that on the third quite slowly. What I mean
is: one wants to read slowly, word for word, in order
to get at the sub-surface values of wisdom, compassion
and irony, and still more slowly to perceive the refine-
ments of language *qua* language, or such Eyckian
minutiae as the "half-moon of glass kept clear before
her by the strokes of the faintly squeaking wiper";
but on the other hand one has to read fast simply
because one wants to know, quite primitively and
justifiably, what is going to happen to the story. The
only way out is to read three times, which we have
done, precisely with the feeling, so well known to an
old iconologist, that one has to move on one level
of interpretation while always being conscious of
two or three others. It may amuse you that—while
we were both proceeding on the "plot" or "story"
level—*The Lorenzo Bunch* cost us two pounds of
apples and a still serviceable alumnium pot because
Dora had clean forgotten that she had put them on
the fire, and that *The Plutocrat* caused a real row
because I was inconsiderate enough to tell her "how
it all came out."

In a way, I am sorry that I am not a critic or
historian of literature. It would be great fun (perhaps
it has been done already) simply to trace the influence
of your characters and social problems on the next
generation of writers. So far as I know, it is really you
who discovered that curious and pathetic struggle for
recognition in "Society," which seems to ruin millions
of lives, as a first-rate epical subject (come to think
of it, in Hamburg or Berlin nobody knew the faces of
the "socially prominent" unless one had happened to
meet them somewhere, there being no "Rotogravure
Section"); and how long it took Mr. [Sinclair] Lewis
to discover the innocent bigness and—historically
speaking—legitimacy of the American "barbarian" as

opposed to the "cultured!" And those wonderful thirteen-year-olds in *The Lorenzo Bunch* and *Gentle Julia* not to mention "Gammire," "offering all he knew, hoping that someone might laugh at him and like him!"

The Plutocrat would seem to be a marvelous example of what you wrote yourself about the "piecemeal appearance of the hero." He actually emerges, growing to overpowering proportions as his figure is reflected in the reluctantly succumbing mind of Mr. Ogle (and the reader), and it is a sheer delight to see how the pace and amplitude of the writing grows proportionally with the growth of the hero. The greatness of *The Lorenzo Bunch,* on the other hand, consists perhaps of the fact that there is no hero, quite literally a "bunch" of human beings, thrown together and reacting on each other—with a hidden nucleus of the divine which comes out only when things go wrong, and most unhappy if they get what they want. The conclusion is one of the most moving things I have ever read.

I feel like your Mr. Rumbin addressing "Mr. Halbert and also Miss Raines" when I thank, and congratulate, Betty Trotter now. Her translation of Mouton's *Epernon* is a masterpiece, and the book itself most amusing, crisp and subtle. One paragraph in the Introduction fills a poor art historian with some misgivings. M. Mouton, the revered translatrix says, "has not sought to 'interpret' the Duke of Epernon psychologically. . . . Mouton shows us the man by his actions." And: "By continually telling us what his man did, instead of weaving a selected portion of his doings into a pattern of inhuman consistency . . . M. Mouton sees to it that we have the stirring truth of the Duke of Epernon." But what is a poor fellow to do if "his man" never "did" anything worth mentioning in his life but merely produced pictures (or, for that matter, symphonies or books) which have to be "interpreted" in order to come into existence? Works, unfortunately, cannot "speak for themselves" as deeds or even letters can just because they emerge from the stream of mere historical "goings-on." He who presumes to write about a maker instead of about a doer has therefore the advantage to write about something that not only was but still is—and has to pay the penalty of being forced to do all the time precisely what Betty Trotter praises M. Mouton for having avoided. Speaking of the Trotter family: that you wanted to give my old book to Mrs. Trotter, that Mrs. Trotter actually bought it, and that you tell me all this is such an accumulation of kindness that I cannot but blush, like Figaro in his most abject moments. Thanks for this liniment on the wounds inflicted by Yale! My own dog, by the way, has founded a family on the Campus. His—I am sorry to say, socially inferior—wife established a nursery in a hollow tree near Blair Arch, and my Jerome, so I am told, stands there knee-deep in puppies, keeping away all other dogs and eating most of the food provided by kind-hearted students. He appears here only about once a week to say hello and in order to maintain his status as a resident of Battle Road.

Hoping with all our hearts for a happy "Wiedersehen" with "you and yours," and with all good wishes imaginable,

Yours as ever devotedly,
Dora and Erwin Panofsky

The Grandeman family, formerly Brooklyn residents, came to Kennebunkport in 1931 as "summer people," after spending several years in Europe: Christian, his wife Elsie, and his two unmarried daughters, Mary and Marian. Even-

tually they made the town their permanent home. For many years Christian Grandeman had tea at "The Floats" almost every afternoon.

Seawood
Kennebunkport, Maine
Thanksgiving '43

Dear Dr. Panofsky:—

Thank you not only for the festal nourishments but for the means to flatten out "my" committee with an exhibition of learnedness. No. I don't mean what you might at first think; I mean I'll be as impressive, in that groove, as it's safe to be when I say "My friend, Dr. Panofsky, kindly supplied me with these pictures and he informs me" etc. etc. etc.

It's a shame how you're quoted by the Trotters, the Burrages, the Grandemans, and Tarkingtons—mostly all wrong. I seem to recall that a part of your summer was busy with the explanation, "No, I didn't say that, I said just the reverse. If you remember I *began* by saying" and so on.

The lady who asked help on her choice, whether the Turner, the Hobbema, or the Holbein, writes me most gratefully. She bought a Corneille de Lyon. I can only hope it is. . . .

Gratefully,
N. B. T.

Frank Atkins helped the Tarkingtons take care of "The Floats," after working for many years at the Yacht Club. Francis Mulberry Chick was Tarkington's chauffeur in Kennebunkport, a 250-pound man who lived on Tarkington property with his wife Edna and his young son Booth. He was a devoted employee from 1930 to 1946, but he refused to install a telephone in his house, arguing that "I do enough for them 'summer people' as 'tis."

The first mention of Suger is premature. Panofsky's Abbot Suger on the Abbey Church of St.-Denis and Its Art Treasures *did not appear until 1946. It is a translation, with commentary, drawings, photographs, and a lengthy introduction of three texts "long familiar to every student of medieval art and civilization": Suger's account of his activities as Abbot, the* Liber de Rebus in Administratione Sua Gestis; *his report on the construction of his new narthex and chevet,* Libellus Alter de Consecratione Ecclesiae Sancti Dionysii; *and one of his* Ordinationes *of 1140 or 1141. The abbey, seven miles from Paris, was founded about 630 by the Merovingian king Dagobert I near the sanctuary that St. Genevieve had allegedly erected in the fifth century above the tomb of the martyr. The Merovingian church, enhanced by the king's sculptor and goldsmith, St. Eloy, was replaced by the Carolingian basilica by 775. Suger did not enter the abbey until 1091. Although of humble origins, he was a tutor and adviser to Louis VI, a distinguished historian and statesman, and, by 1122, the Abbot of St. Denis. Fourteen years later he began the new abbey church which "still deserves to be called," according to Panofsky, "the parent monument of all Gothic cathedrals." This monograph, a masterful recreation of the abbot as well as the aesthetics of Gothic style, Panofsky dedicated to Booth Tarkington.*

[Kennebunkport]
Sept. 30—'44

Dear Dr. Panofsky:

I most gratefully thank you for the two books.
Thus far I haven't been able to get at them—being
read aloud to's a slow process and other works are
slowly moving from previous beginnings. I did a few
pages of Heinrich Mann with my own impeded eyes
and was a bit set aback by Germans who speak semi-
American; but that anomalous effort can be side-
tracked, of course; I realize the intentions to obtain
a vernacular effect. It does "just the opposite"—makes
one stop to think about the author and his struggle,
not unlike that of Victor Hugo who named an English-
man "Tom-Jim-Jack" in order to make him absolutely
British. I *do* wish to arrive at the German-ness of his
book and won't let my small discomfort deter me.
I'll write you when I've got ahead.

Your hearts would bleed could you come to the
"Floats" these afternoons. Betty poured bad plaster
into the molds of her uncle's head. Digging it out, half-
hardened, tiny bit by bit, makes even Figaro weep.
Mr. Noble's help (vocal) is worse than negligible, and
old Frank's advice doesn't advance the work; he spends
most of the time apologizing for offering inept sug-
gestions.

"The Burrages" blew in last night. You'll agree
that they *do* blow in, I think. Kennebunkport therefore now seems more like itself; but that doesn't
reward us for what we lost by your departure. We have
a little Mozart left for our evenings, it's true; but
the afternoon vacancies at "coffee time" are pathetic.
Two figures, first silhouetted against the light of the
opened farther door, then developing into form and
color as they briskly approach the verandah, are
always expectantly awaited—but they *arrive* not at
all! It's always Mr. Noble.

Of "news" I can give you nothing stimulating.
Chick has lost his potatoes because of a wrong rainfall,
and his spaniel has a sore eye. Despondency is pon-
derous. He figgas them potatoes cost him $25, not
counting his labor. How often he has told us this I
will not burden you by computing. The noblest of
tomato crops does not balance his account with Mother
Nature; man was not made for happiness.

Suger will come in '45; we can look forward to that
year for *another* blessing, then. We think often of
your prodigious little man.

We hope you'll be disappointed, evanescently, on
November 6th; but upon both of you our blessings.
Next summer we look to have a boat to offer as induce-
ment for the Panofskys' return. A handkerchief waving from a high rock to welcome the whale-chasers
home is a pretty sight.

Faithfully your neighbor,
Booth Tarkington

*Israel and Abby Maling were a well-known Ken-
nebunkport couple long before the Tarkingtons
or Burrages moved to town, working at various
odd-jobs including opening and closing the
houses owned by the "summer people." During
their 1944 visit, the Panofskys occupied the Mc-
Kinney house, a tiny cottage near Ocean Avenue
and within sight of "The Floats."*

Kennebunkport
October 14—'44

Dear Dr. Panofsky:

Betty broke the news—the intended dedication—
but I couldn't write of my astonished gratification yesterday as that was Friday the Thirteenth and we had

with us neither Suger nor any of his devout to exorcise the probable ill, or evil, that could befall the book were I so reckless.

The astonishment just mentioned I think you'll comprehend. It arises not because we'd previously doubted your good will toward your coastal friends; but out of a sense of the appropriate—so intricately a work of scholarship to carry the name of an old party so preposterously unlearned.

All the more profound, naturally, is that person's gratitude and all the more agreeably is his vanity enlarged and sweetened. To be brought at one stroke into public association with Panofsky and the great Abbot of St. Denis—I shall expect (but probably not receive) more deference from even F. Mulberry Chick. Here I *must* interrupt myself to tell you about the car in which a "petting party" was suspected by you and Mrs. Panofsky—the automobile outside your house on the night of the pilfering. It contained our Chick, no more and no less, and in a condition of slumber. He knew that we were intending to join in a merry-making at your cottage; that we meant to arrive on foot and that he was expected to bring us home, later— but he became confused (no difficult matter) about the date and came for us Saturday night, waited, waited, waited, slept, slept, slept, finally awoke and drove home. The pilferers were the little Caron boy and comrades.

How is this known? Your summer house curator, the aged Maling. He returned to these his native rocks for a visit last week, brought to the "Floats" as a gift the portrait of a cow once the source of trouble between himself and Mrs. Maling, and spent the whole afternoon telling us many things, all of them disconnected. He carried a new cane—no, not a new one but a very, very old one; and he told us how he obtained it. He had long known an aged woman of

Roxbury, Mass. who used a cane because of arthritis. She, being dead, would have no further use for such a utensil; so he called at her house, explained his need and was sympathetically given this new-old cane.

That was his *theme*, repeated with embroidering variations. What had happened to his *former* cane was lightly and briefly touched upon, a mere secondary passage. Leaving a subsidiary Boston Post Office he thought the soldier behind him had courteously opened the door for him, but the military man spoke to him crossly: "Whatcha mean, walkin' out ahead of a *soldier?*"

Mr. Maling: "Talk that way, you're no credit to the Flag."

Soldier: "Aw, to hell with the Flag!"

"When he says that," continued Mr. Maling, "I hit him over the head with my cane and broke it in two. So I hit him again with the piece of it I held in my hand and then throwed it away. They was twenty or thutty people watchin' us, but none of 'em said nothin', so he went on down the street and I didn't have no cane."

If I speak of the dedication gaily, be sure it's not lightly. I couldn't receive an honor more distinguished or one I'd value more highly; but that's only one of the reasons for a deeply stirred appreciation. The others I safely leave to Mrs. Panofsky's interpretation. She knows how eloquently I'd *like* to say "Thank you!" and how stumblingly we males make our feelings known at such times.

Most permanently in gratefulness, I am

> Your proud debtor,
> Booth Tarkington

On October 3, Betty Trotter had written to Panofsky to say "Mr. T. is writing a Rumbin story" and needs help. (The character Mr. Rumbin, the art dealer, was based on the two men who sold Tarkington paintings, David and Abris Silberman of New York; he first appeared in The Saturday Evening Post *in 1936 and a year later in the novel* Rumbin Galleries.) *Miss Trotter outlined the problem in detail: "Mr. Rumbin, from a propensity to show off, has blackened the reputation of an objet d'art about which he knows absolutely nothing. Mr. T. would like to have his objet (one unassailable in integrity) be one of Suger's from St. Denis—if you don't object. . . . If you acquiesce, could you help about what the objet could plausibly be? . . . Could the objet be (legendarily) something of Dagobert's? A chalice of amber? (I don't remember any mention of amber in Suger's unctious itemizations.) Set in a gold case—rubies? A verse of Suger's on it? And would you mind its being brought out, to complete Mr. Rumbin's discomfiture, that your translation describes the objet?"*

Panofsky suggested the gondola of St. Eloy, a boat or "navette" (employed for holding the grains of incense) carved from prase or jade, and decorated with cloisonné enamel, formerly in the treasury of the abbey church. According to legend it had been made by St. Eloy himself, but in 1804 it was stolen from the Cabinet des Médailles in the Bibliothèque Nationale and never recovered.

Dear Dr. Panofsky:—

Yesterday other gratitudes so preoccupied me that the one for the gondola was omitted—and you'd gone

"The Floats," Kennebunkport, Maine   *Photograph by Patrick W. Grace*

Interior of "The Floats"

Erwin Panofsky, c. 1940

Booth Tarkington, c. 1938

"Seawood," Kennebunkport, Maine

97 Battle Road, Princeton, New Jersey

Photograph by Everett Sce

to the pains of completing the description with
elaborate illustrations!

Precisely what I needed. I'll send you the *ms*
of the little story when it's completed and you'll see.

We owe (also, also, and also) to you and Mrs.
Panofsky the inestimable gift of eyes freshened to
perceive the wonders of this neighborhood anew.
When our earlier years of such perception came to the
full I needed two whole books plus many shorter expressions to relieve my soul of the pressure. Then what
was wild began to be commonplace. I became as a
beetle living in the treasure room of the Caliph,
unaware of rubies.

Now, alert again, I've arrived unto a local scene
of delightful crime—a bit of landscape so spicy that
lovely things may come of movements thereon. The
matter is delicate, higher than Chicks being involved.
I could impart it by word of mouth only, when we
meet—and, as life is made of excitements dulled in
their culminations, by then it may have lost edge and
be but moldy Roquefort. However, at the present
moment we're enriched by the problem: Who Stole
Another Stone Fence? How secret the affair is you
may guess when I mention that presently the Burrages
will be here to lunch and I dare not whisper of it
to them—unless they already know!

St. Eloy's blessing be upon you.

Again gratefully,
Booth Tarkington

*This letter to Betty Trotter is included here be-
cause it is an important prelude to the two long
and serious letters which follow.*

*Wendell Willkie waged a vigorous campaign
against Franklin Roosevelt in 1940 but lost the*

presidential election by almost five million votes. During the next four years he was the major spokesman within his party for international cooperation and an end to isolationism. His best-selling book, One World, *appeared in 1943. Conservative Republicans, however, would not support his platform, and when he lost the Wisconsin primaries he withdrew from the race. In August of that year he suffered a heart attack; one month before the presidential election he died.*

Robert Gilbert Vansittart was an undersecretary in the British Foreign Office during the 1930s and chief diplomatic adviser to Prime Minister Neville Chamberlain. For many years he spent all his energies warning Britain of the Nazi threat, but his efforts, particularly with Chamberlain, were in vain. He retired in 1941.

The "events of and after July 20" were the attempt by Colonel Claus Schenk Graf von Stauffenberg to assassinate Hitler by planting a bomb at his headquarters in East Prussia, the execution of many of the men implicated in the plot, and the consequent destruction of the German army's independence.

97 Battle Road
Princeton, N. J.
November 1, 1944

Dear Betty,

The first of a month is a good day to pay debts, and I, too, should like to seize upon the opportunity to thank you and Mr. Tarkington for no less than three letters—one from you and two from him—which I should have answered much earlier. I am more than grateful for Mr. Tarkington's gracious willingness to

accept the dedication of *Suger,* and if he thinks that
the little book is worth having I shall not care much
for what the reviewers will say. I really feel very thankful toward both of you.

Also, I am enormously pleased to hear that Mr.
Tarkington can use the "gondola of St. Eloy," and you
can imagine my curiosity and anticipation as to what
he will do with it. After I had written you about it
I secured two more little bits of information: first,
that such "gondolas" are still in use in many Catholic
churches, that they are professionally referred to as
"boats," and that they serve to hold the grains of
incense that go into the censers. Second, that the
burglars of 1804 smuggled their loot, or at least part
of it, into England by the wonderful device of hiding
it within a plaster cast of the upper half of the *Laocoön,*
precisely as the Borgia Pearl in Sherlock Holmes'
Six Napoleons. I don't know whether or not these
additional touches can be used, but I pass them on
just the same.

I was glad that life—or at least professional life—
in the last three weeks consisted entirely of proofreading, partly for *Suger* and partly for the second
printing of Dürer, for I would have hardly been able
to concentrate upon something more productive. We
are both very much excited and, frankly, distracted
by the turn the Campaign has taken. You will hardly
know it, but the head of the Republican Committee of
Pennsylvania has seen fit to distribute millions of
violently antisemitic pamphlets in this neighborhood,
and the slogan "Well, these boys will cease to be that
way after election" did not work so very well in
Germany. It is really a great pity that Willkie is dead
—though perhaps not so great a pity as that he was
not nominated—and it must be hard, for those who
loved him, now to vote for just those two men who
were responsible for his political liquidation. He

seemed to grow in defeat, and it is one of the major tragedies that he had to die just now. In retrospect, it would seem that those who voted against him last time did so because they did not believe that he meant what he said—and that very many of those who did vote for him also did so because they did not believe that he meant what he said. When it turned out that he had been serious all the time his own party turned against him and thereby deprived his former opponents of the chance to support him now. What an irony!

Some people seem to think that he planned, after his defeat in Wisconsin, to found a kind of liberal party mainly recruited from the more progressive elements within the Republican Party—as now his former manager R[ussell W.] Davenport might want to do. I have thought about this idea a good deal, and find it terribly complicated. On the one hand, there is, of course, no denying that the present party lines are all wrong. There are, as you wrote, good men and true on both sides, and bad men and untrue as well. Although I am forced to vote Democratic once more I do not feel that I "belong" to the Party of Mr. [Martin] Dies or Mr. [Robert] Reynolds. And although you are forced to vote Republican I do not feel that you "belong" to the Party of Ham Fish (and even, I cannot help thinking after your words about Willkie, Mr. Dewey). It would be an attractive thought if there were a party on which we could agree. But then again, if this dream were to come true, what would happen? Such a new party would drain the old ones of their best elements (best in the sense on which we agree without much definition), but it would not be strong enough to win the next election. As a result, whichever of the two old parties would win would be able to do infinitely more harm than is the case now. For, while at present the "bad" men on either

side prevent the "good" ones from going ahead one
hundred percent, the contrary is also true: the "good"
ones prevent the "bad" ones from going ahead one
hundred percent, too. It all boils down to the fact that
the *terrena civitas* is not destined to be perfect, and
that every attempt to make it so is frowned upon by
the Highest Authority. On the whole, it would seem,
the two-party-system is a sheer blessing in comparison
to the multi-party system of France and pre-Hitler
Germany, and the one really valid argument for a
"change" is simply that the prolonged absence of such
a change tends to undermine the workings of the
two-party-system as such and may lead the protest
vote to crystallize around the Gerald Smiths instead
of a "regular" opposition candidate. If only Willkie
had been nominated and had lived!

Speaking of "protest vote": one of the most frequent
objections to Vansittart is that Germany before
Hitler had about three million Communist voters,
from which it is concluded that there must be that
many anti-Nazis. Nothing could be "wronger." The
simple fact is that the protest vote in Germany simply
had to go outside the "coalition" which formed the
government—either Nazi or Communist, and that it
was mostly a matter of pure accident whether a person
dissatisfied with the government *in esse* voted the one
way or the other; my guess is that at least two thirds
of those who voted Communist in 1932 are now happily
absorbed by the Nazis, and the fact that (as I ventured
to foretell in Kennebunkport) the events of and after
July 20, 1944 have strengthened rather than weakened
the German resistance would seem to bear out Vansittart's tenet that the Nazi movement was and is a
people's, and not a Junker's or industrialist's movement
—although the Junkers and industrialists "took it
up" in the hope of controlling it.

44 Forgive me for writing almost as I talk, viz., too much, and may the Holy Martyrs be with you and Mr. T.

> Yours as ever,
> Pan & Dora

[Kennebunkport]
Nov. 5—'44

Dear Dr. Panofsky:

"I write in haste" because of your saying that you and Mrs. Panofsky are distressed by an antisemitic ebullition. Take my word for it: you can laugh at it. Nothing of that sort can do you the slightest harm unless *you* let it make you apprehensive or hurt your feelings. Antisemitism in this country is the most futile of gestures and *can't* be more. Naturally, after what happened in Germany, I know how such a gesture would loom large in your minds, disturbing your imaginations; but don't *waste* anxiety on such impotences as mere nose-thumbing which is all the stuff amounts to. And a *political* anti-*anything* is worth just as much as the boy-actor Orson Wells's (I knew his uncle, whose name was Wells not Welles) proclaiming "Nobody not an idiot will vote for Dewey."

It's impossible for me to take seriously any worry over antisemitism in this country. The worry is an *imported* one.

I've been of an "outcast race" myself, at times—enough to make me incredulously half resentful, half amused. The manifestations were "Eastern," because I came from the Midwest—Indiana in particular—and am a Hoosier "We never think of you as from Indiana" was said to me consolingly more than once in my youth. Sometime I'd like to tell you of the spirit in which my first novel was written—and the result, somewhat paralysing to a writer in his twenties. However, I was better able to understand the feeling animating the old cartoonist, Hy Mayer, when he told me, one night, long ago, that a friend of his had said to him, "I never think of you as a Jew." "That showed he thought of it," Hy said. I can't recall even *hearing* of "antisemitism" until I'd been quite a while out of Princeton. At home, sometimes, one had heard "He's a Jew" just as one heard "He's from Ohio." Indiana had the noble family of Judah; my brother-in-law's sister was Mrs. John Judah; and an intimate of our family group, as he was of other "prominent citizen" family groups, was Nathan Morris who loved to tell "Jew stories" and, after laughing through a successful life, died heroically and was mourned by the whole city. At Exeter, Sam Weiss was a member of the school-fraternity to which I belonged—the most influential member. I recall, vaguely, somebody's saying, "Sam's a Jew, isn't he?" and somebody else, "I don't know—yes, I believe he is." At Princeton, my classmate, Phil King, was the captain of both the football and the baseball teams. That wasn't the reason why he wasn't spoken of as a Jew; nobody noticed whether he was or not. I visited another classmate, Saxe Kalisky, in New York and had a happy time with his delightful family. Telling about it on my return I was asked incuriously by my room-mate, "Jewish, aren't they?" and answered truthfully, "They may be—I don't know."

I'm detailing this to give you the *"typical* American" thought and feeling—which is *still* typical. Indeed it's *fundamental* and will prevail so long as we have a Republic. "Gangs" in cities don't like people who differ in appearance or customs or heritage from themselves. In Boston there's been Jew-baiting by hoodlums. In Indianapolis there have been gang fights between Irish and Negroes. In many smaller towns, South Side fights North Side, etc. Chinamen have been stoned for sport, Jewish boys joining in. Hoodlumism is hoodlumism; it isn't antisemitism.

46   There's something that *counterfeits* antisemitism
and I have had a personal experience of it. Years ago
a hotel stood where the Casino is now, here at the 'Port.
It just happened that the same "crowd" of people
occupied that hotel year after year, and they were the
most offensively ill-mannered group I ever observed—
and one *had* to observe them because they shouldered
one off the board-sidewalks we had then, made
"Miller's" and the dime-movie so noisy the "old
patrons" stayed away, and they just "*took*" the beach.
Most of them were from Brooklyn and most of them
were Jews. The latter fact had *nothing* to do with
the feeling I had that they were "spoiling Kennebunkport," except for themselves; and I joined a group of
summer residents and "natives" who bought the hotel.
(It burned to the ground almost immediately! Irony,
but accidental.)

That wasn't antisemitism; it was anti-Brooklyn,
anti-barbarian, and may have been snobbish just as
another such expensive episode was two years ago when
a few of us bought the lot you looked out upon this
summer. Overnight cabins would have filled it if we
hadn't. I wish that, too, we could have kept Dock
Square as it used to be. If the "natives" who've *changed*
it happened to be of Jewish descent, such a wish (if
acted upon) *might* be called antisemitism. It *wouldn't*
be that, it would be snobbishness maybe, as I've just
admitted; but the "antisemitism" would be of the
counterfeit kind.

Politicians' propaganda makes a *try* at *every* possible thing. There are some people everywhere who
"don't like Jews" just as there are people who "don't
like the Irish," or the English, or South Americans,
or red hair, or Prohibitionists, or Catholics, or Baptists,
or anything under the sun. Antisemitism of the counterfeit kind can be either hoodlumism or snobbism.
I give you my word, as an old American who knows

75-years-worth of his fellow-countrymen, you can laugh at antisemitism just as cheerfully as I laugh at anti-Hoosierism. Both are Boojums, and for God's sake, don't let *your* Boojum disturb a single moment of your lives—not in the United States! The Ku Klux Klan? Its great strength was in "my" two states, Indiana and Maine. In Maine it was Chick: hates Catholics. The "Catholics" (French) brought Indians to scalp the English settlers. *He* doesn't know *that*; but from father to son the Chicks hate "Catholics." In Indiana the K. K. K. was partly real estate, partly political machine, partly a country boy's wish to wear a hood, mask, and gown. Real estate? To keep negroes from moving into "select" areas of the towns. Political? Used by both parties as a "machine." The whole thing broke up when the leaders were exposed—getting $13. out of every $15. it cost the initiate! The *inside* of the K. K. K. was a "con game." To "sum up," you *may*, at times (and so may I) run into "social embarrassments"; but they will be petty. I once heard some women in a hotel talking shrilly; they were in the next room and didn't know how thin was the partition. They indignantly agreed that they would *not* sit at the same table with persons who pronounced watuh and buttuh as "wat-*ur*" and "but-*tur*." I was the offensive beast; they'd been put at my table. They felt contaminated by Indiana. Is there anybody, or any "type," in the world to whom some other body or "type" does not "object"? In Germany the objectee couldn't laugh at the objector. Here he can and does—except when being called such names as "the greedy few," "economic royalists," and "princes of privilege" etc. injures his *business*. *Then* he naturally gets pretty sore.

About being "forced" to vote for Dewey, as you feel you're forced to vote for F. D. R. I *ought* to explain that I LEAP to vote for Dewey—ineffectually

I strongly fear. "It's a long story"—too long for this interminable letter—and would be an autobiography with a preface intricately historical. To hint an outline I might quote a bit from a broadcast heard yesterday. The speaker mentioned the Arch of Titus which maintained the fiction S. P. Q. R. a hundred years after Pressure Groups had begun to impose Emperors and reduce the Senate to yes-men. Until F. D. R. all the presidents in my lifetime have maintained Equality Before the Law, the Constitution, Personal Liberty Under the Law, the Two-Party System, the Three-Functional System—legislative, judicial, and executive —and the *soul* as well as the form of a Republic. In 1936, F. D. R. said of certain citizens he wished regarded as a hated *Class*: "In my second administration I would like to show myself their Master." This was from the heart, and strange to hear in a country that until then (after the Abolition of Slavery) knew no Masters, not even of criminals in prison. He made the Congress his tool, strove to destroy the Supreme Court by means of that tool, and *has* made it and the Dept. of Justice his agents. Washington's aversion to a third term came from his forebodings—someday a too popular president *could* become a Ruler. F. D. R. *wants* a *Fourth*! In brief: if all the blessings of heaven came to a people through such processes I should abhor both the processes and the blessings; they end the Republic and foreshadow a coming tyrant, a "Master"—however dimly. The Leader of a one-party system is a Dictator, willy-nilly.

"Such considerations," to my mind, outweigh everything else, and Dewey is a *law* man. The change would break up the mechanism that threatens the country with totalitarianism, State Socialism, [one-]man rule. Dewey's a charmless person, not sleek as a politician, not adroit with words; but he's bed-rock for the Republic. I pretty well know the kind of man

they both are. I've had friends quite a lot like F. D. R.
—mostly writers and actors—and others *very* like
Dewey, businessmen and lawyers. It was always safer
to have the latter run the club: they kept it out of debt
and in accordance with the rules.

Alas, poor Willkie! Too young departing, he left
his everything unfinished and, I believe, *not thought-
out* completely. He had hopes rather than clear plans
for the world—generous hopes *some* day to be realized.
From tones in his voice and expressions of his face I
know what he thought of F. D. R.—not that Willkie
didn't speak *out* with passionate vehemence "off the
record"—"We've *got* to get that gang out of Washington!" But of F. D. R. personally, those tones and
expressions were most eloquent. They were the look
and sound of a man engaged with a wily antagonist
who has more than once slyly out-tricked him, cannot
for an instant be trusted to "fight fair" and must be
"watched like a cat." The last time we saw Willkie was
when he came to speak to Indiana, the winter of '43-'44.
His talk was to be broadcast; but the first thing W. said
after reaching our house was, "That man in Washington waited until my date here was set and couldn't be
changed. Then he grabbed a 'nation-wide hook-up'
for a Fireside Chat at that hour. It's like him."

There! This is all to make *me* clear—not to
propagandize *you*, which it wouldn't, and you'll have
voted before it reaches you, so my innocence of such
an attempt is proven. I'll add only that today your
eyes, if here, would be rewarded by a deeply white
Kennebunkport and a sea invisible behind the driving
ghosts of snow. Mildred upheaved with an Auction for
the War Fund to which Mrs. Dwight and Mr. Parsons
contributed objects of such value that M. declined to
have them put up to fishermen bidders. She accepted
our piano but withdrew it also—until dealers should
be goaded to act against one another. Mr. Noble is

"keeping house" for Mrs. Littlefield (who's away) and must feed her dog hurtly because when he said he didn't know what to offer the animal, Betty suggested "Oh, just salt water!" Her reference was to what he gave the "Floats" pigeons one year when we had such birds and he signed up to care for them.

Otherwise all is well—or at least as well as destiny permits in case, as I suspect Mr. Roosevelt will have been triumphantly re-seated when you read this verbiage which seems desirous to compete with Dr. Theodore Meyer Greene's voluminousness.

Faithfully,
Booth Tarkington

Princeton, N. J.
November 11, 1944

Dear Mr. Tarkington,

I can hardly tell you how touched we both are by your kindness in spending so much time, labor and thought on assuaging what must have struck you as unnecessary misgivings, and on making us see the causes of your and your friends' convictions. We are deeply grateful and have been attentive readers. And I feel that the best thing to do is to answer with equal frankness and, as Suger would say, *eodem spiritu*. I beg your leave to use the typewriter because I would not like to subject you or Betty to more than the usual amount of my handwriting.

Concerning the question of antisemitism, I am convinced, not only by your examples but also by personal observation, that you are perfectly right in diagnosing it, in its present form, as something very different from its European manifestations—hoodlumism on the one hand, and snobbery on the other. I therefore share your belief that there is no great danger, for the time being and perhaps even for the future, of its becoming "organized." There are indeed several safety valves here that are absent from the European scene. First, there is the indisputable fact that, as you say, the Jews are only one of several minority groups and therefore less likely to be made the one and only scapegoat in times of stress; it was perhaps one of the reasons for the ultimate failure of the Ku Klux Klan that it tried to take on too many minority groups at the same time. Second, the snobbish or "social" form of discrimination is in itself a kind of protection. The European Ghetto, unknown until *after* the first concerted persecution, *protected* the Jews in segregating them, and it is no accident that the subsequent persecutions were always preceded by periods of relative liberalism. The great Spanish persecution of the 15th and 16th century followed an era in which Jews were almost completely accepted, and in pre-Hitler Germany social discrimination of the "restricted clientele" type was virtually unknown; also mixed marriages were infinitely more frequent, especially between Jews and nobility (witness my own family tree) than they are here. Therefore I am, personally, rather in favor of the "snobbish" form of discrimination; for as long as it remains snobbish, it is less likely to merge with the hoodlumish variety, and it is only the fusion of these two, sanctioned by a sort of philosophy, which transforms discrimination and sporadic outbreaks of violence into organized persecution. In this campaign, now, there were in fact some attempts to bring about this very fusion—not very successful and perhaps not without some temptation by the C. I. O. itself (which might have done better to find some leader other than the otherwise apparently quite decent Mr. Hillman), but hard to overlook entirely. A well-known lady in Princeton actually tried to convince me that I ought to persuade my Jewish fellow-citizens to vote for Dewey in order to prevent a "further rise of antisemitism" (it was the same lady, though, who told President Dodds that, if he expected financial support from her and her friends, he should fire all the "reds" on his faculty and, when asked whom she meant, defined them as "all those people who announced they are going to vote for Roosevelt"). Concerning that Philadelphia leaflet that I mentioned to Betty, I am sorry to say that I threw away the copy that fell into my hands (it showed portraits of Roosevelt and Hillman juxtaposed with portraits of Jewish gangsters, and the text was such that it was banned by the Postmaster). I am including, however, a report on the Senate investigation of the matter. I have no way of checking up on this report, but since it refers to the Senate Campaign Expenditures Committee's subcommittee and Senator Ball by name, it sounds rather authentic. I am the last to overestimate the importance of such phenomena, especially during a Presidential campaign. I only found them disagreeable because—if the Philadelphia report is correct—this kind of thing was, so far as I know for the first time, prompted on what might be called a policy-making level. However, this Jewish problem is really quite secondary. It seems to be the historical mission of the Jews to contribute, like Socrates' gadfly, to the progress of civilization by being a perennial nuisance, and the responsibility for the results rests neither with the gadfly nor with the horse. The thing that matters is the general problem of government, and this has two aspects: the special situation in October/November 1944, and the basic principle.

So far as 1944 is concerned, I am still convinced that—regardless of the two candidates' objective merits—the choice of Mr. Roosevelt was fortunate because of its repercussions abroad. The Germans may have been mistaken, as Betty writes, in thinking that Mr. Dewey's election would make a material difference.

But they would certainly have thought so, or rather
did think so, and, in view of Mr. Dewey's and Mr.
Landon's published statements (not to mention Mrs.
Luce's "He lied us into this war") not without reason.
Even this *thought* would have gone a long way to keep
them going. From the European point of view, defeat
in an election means repudiation of the candidate *in
toto*; they will never understand (and it took me
many years to understand) that here a candidate can
be defeated "on one issue" while his basic policies
in other fields remain unaffected. From the German
point of view Roosevelt is the arch-enemy. His defeat
by *any* opponent, of whom they know little or nothing,
would have meant to them only one thing: the Americans are sick of the war. They might have found out
later that such is not the case, but that would have
taken much time because they would have been told
that the change could not come quite of a sudden;
until then they would have been fortified by hope, and
even in modern warfare such psychological factors
count very heavily (I remember our tri-cornered
conversation on the Floats, when Mr. Murdock was
there, as to the probable effect of the events of and
after July 20, and I am sorry to say that I was right in
conjecturing that they would strengthen rather than
weaken the German will to resist). Conversely, our
Allies, rightly or wrongly, consider Roosevelt as the
great symbol or even source of anti-Nazi energies and
knowing about as much about Mr. Dewey as do
the Germans, would have been disappointed and
doubtful in the same measure as the Germans would
have been hopeful. They, too, might have found out
that they were wrong, but that, too, would have taken
time. Added to this is the commonplace considera-
tion that a defeated Government would have been
unable to conduct negotiations with any amount of
authority, so that there would have been, on the

diplomatic front, a kind of interregnum of at least three months.

It was, quite apart from personal preference, out of considerations like these that a great number of our friends here and in New York voted for Roosevelt this time though they had never done so before. It was, I am told, this independent vote (plus the soldier vote) that swung the State of New Jersey and accounted for the increase of Roosevelt's plurality (as compared to 1940) in New York. The Hague machine in New Jersey produced 30,000 votes less than in 1940, but all over the place Independent Committees were formed (the one in Princeton under the guidance of none other than Mrs. Allan Marquand, who dislikes Roosevelt and had never voted for him in all her life); and one of my Institute colleagues, likewise disliking Roosevelt, made his decision to vote for him just the same on the basis of Mr. Dewey's speech in New York re German resistance. As a result, Princeton, though still going to Dewey, did so with a plurality of only 528 votes as against several thousands in previous elections, and this in a district almost as barren of "regular" Democrats and what you may call "retainers" of the Federal Government as Maine.

This brings me to the general aspects of the question. Dear Mr. Tarkington, I think that I can understand and share your and your friends' fears for the two-party system (which, from all historical experience, is the only workable one), and that I am not blind to the dangers in the rise of a great class psychologically and economically dependent upon the Federal Government, and in the emergence of Labor as a political instead of merely economical force. Further, you know so infinitely more about conditions in the United States (I still feel like Heinrich Wölfflin who, when asked whether his was a Basel family, answered: "No, we did not come here until 1567, but we are getting accustomed"), that I cannot presume to say anything except in terms of the universal development as I seem to see it. And this is the following: the one thing that has proved impracticable in *every* sphere of human endeavor is consistency or, what amounts to the same thing, a radically one-sided solution. Aristotle was, basically, a "monist" in that he refused to accept a substantial dichotomy between "matter" and "form" and, therefore, between body and soul. But, being a great man, he permitted himself to be inconsistent in one respect: he acknowledged that in the human soul there was something foreign to and, in a measure, independent of the body—something "that comes in by the door." His followers, such as Aristoxenos, were quick to eliminate this inconsistency: they made the whole soul a function of the body ("much as the sound of a lyre is a function of its strings")— and thereby reduced "monism" *ad absurdum.* Descartes, conversely, was a "dualist" in that he insisted on a dichotomy between *substance pensante* and *substance étendue,* and, therefore, between mind and body. But he, too, permitted himself to be inconsistent in that he claimed that the pineal gland, though a part of the body and thus of the *substance étendue,* could yet be influenced, in some way or other, by thought and will and thereby establish a functional connection between the mind and the body after all. Again it was a small follower, named Geulincx, who was dissatisfied: he made Descartes consistent in denying any such connection ("*I* cannot lift a glass from the table—my body does it and my soul looks on"), and thereby, again, reduced "dualism" *ad absurdum.*

Similarly, it would seem, there is an eternal conflict between too radically one-sided concepts of government which we may call, for want of better and briefer expressions, individual freedom and collectivistic regimentation. Carried to extremities, *both* principles defeat themselves, the former leading to anarchy with "everyone for himself, the devil take the hindmost, and the strongest coming out on top"—the latter to the ant hill with "no one for himself, the devil take all of us, and Heil to the Führer." All history is an attempt to balance these two conflicting principles with varying emphasis on the one and the other.

Now, it would seem that *colonial* conditions permit, for a very long time, an *almost* complete realization of the ideal of individual freedom. With space and resources unlimited, and the pioneer coping with all situations in his own right, every individual or little group can be permitted to look after themselves without much, if any, interference by a central authority. And, given a certain amount of basic goodness in the human makeup, nobody is much harmed. But as the *colonial* situation transforms itself into a "normal" one ("normal" in the sense of the older European civilizations), this unrestrained exercise of individual freedom begins, of necessity, to create great hardships for the weaker members of the community, especially when such weaker members are imported *en masse* in the course of progressing industrialization. For those born and bred in the traditional atmosphere of freedom, every attempt to regulate the ensuing problems by government interference must mean an intolerable attempt at regimentation. But I should venture to believe that such attempts are the inevitable consequence of the fact that the U.S. has definitively and irrevocably outgrown a period in which it could still enjoy the advantages of a great colony, and entered one in which it has to put up with the disadvantages of a "normal" great country. The whole New Deal legislation that seems so offensive to the free and individualistic American, even much more, has been introduced into Germany, France and England between 1890 and 1915; labor rights, "social security" (and I can still remember the campaign pictures of 1936 showing the "dog tag" everyone was supposed to wear upon receiving a social security number), and even socialized medicine.

Now I am not attempting to convince you or anyone that all these things are *desirable* or to deny that they are potentially dangerous (they worked out well in England but not in Germany). I am only trying to say that, objectionable though they must appear to many Americans deeply imbued with the original spirit of freedom and individualism, they were not brought into being by Mr. Roosevelt out of sheer wickedness and lust for power. In my opinion he tried to *shape* the inevitable instead of opposing it. Of course, he loves power, and power is, as Jacob Burckhardt says, "evil." But power is, at the same time, the only instrument of action as well as destruction—just as knives and saws are the instruments of the surgeon as well as of the sadist (and there is a psychological theory according to which a man entirely free from sadistic inclinations would never *become* a surgeon). It is extremely unfair to say that the great individualistic banker or industrialist is just "greedy"; he can, on the contrary, be extraordinarily generous, and many of those who oppose the New Deal would have no reason to do so from a purely financial point of view. But they, too, love power. Henry Ford was always willing to give his workers *higher* wages than did his competitors, but he did not want them to be in a position to *demand* the *same* wages as they received from his competitors. He was willing to pay five dollars a day to the kind of workman he liked, but he hated the idea of somebody's telling him that he had to pay four dollars to the kind of workman he did not like. I can see that he must conceive of any law compelling him to do just this as an infringement upon his liberty; but I cannot help seeing, on the other hand, that the absence of such a law is an infringement upon the liberty of the workman. As I said, I do not believe that the individualistic, or patriarchal, or—to revert to the former expression, "colonial"—order of things is in any way "worse" than its opposite (carried to extremities, both concepts are absurd, and my personal sympathies are with, let us say, Holland in the 17th century); but I do feel that it began to become anachronistic as soon and in proportion as this continent ceased to be radically different and independent from the rest of the world.

Concerning the personal faults and virtues of Mr. Roosevelt, I must confess ignorance. For the reasons mentioned in the first part of this interminable letter I should have voted for him *this year* even if an Archangel had been running against him (while, at the same time, I can fully appreciate the point of view of a Princetonian who said that he would have refused to vote *for* an Archangel had this Archangel been running for a fourth term). But I do not know of Mr. Roosevelt any more than can be learned from published material accessible to all, that is to say, very little. On the basis of this limited knowledge, however, I cannot conceive of him as a would-be tyrant or dictator. In the first place, he has a sense of humor, and a tyrant or dictator with a sense of humor is a contradiction in terms. In the second place, the very style of his speeches and writings, as it hits the ear of an old philologist, seems to reveal a genuinely humanistic attitude. So strong was this "stylistic" feeling in my mind, or ear, that the wording of that sentence from Roosevelt's Madison Square Garden speech of 1936, as quoted in your letter, struck me as strange or even incongruous—much as a patch of violet would strike me in a Raphael. So I looked it up in the *Public Papers and Addresses*, Vol. V, p. 568, and there is indeed a characteristic difference between the phrase as you remember it and the authentic version. The latter does not speak of a *class of citizens* of whom Mr. R. would like to *be* the master, but rather of certain *social evils,* defined as "monopoly, speculation, reckless banking, class antagonism, war profiteering" which he would like to *meet* their master: "I should like to have it said of my first Administration that in it the forces of selfishness and lust for power met their match. I should like to have it said of my second Administration that in it these forces met their master." I suppose that, from the point of view of the extreme individualist, the authentic version is bad enough. But I do not feel that it evinces a thinking in terms of master and slaves.

Not for a moment, dear Mr. Tarkington, do I attempt to convince you or Betty that I am "right." I merely try to explain to you, as to one whom I so sincerely admire and respect, why it is not possible for me to admit that I am "wrong." Perhaps we are looking at the same object through the same telescope, only from opposite ends—and only history will reduce, or enlarge, the object to its real proportions.

I feel much embarrassed to inflict upon you such an enormous, dogmatic sounding document in questionable English and unsupported by much factual knowledge. But I know you will pardon me, and I do hope that you will continue to look upon other efforts as Dr. Johnson did upon those of the Rev. Hugh Blair of whom he said: "The dog is a Scotchman, and a Presbyterian, and everything he should not be, but I was the first to praise his sermons."

With our warmest wishes and many kind remembrances,

Ever gratefully yours,
Erwin Panofsky

The speech writers Tarkington refers to were, of course, only three among the many who worked for President Roosevelt. Charles Michelson was a publicist for the Democratic National Committee. Thomas G. Corcoran, protégé of Felix Frankfurter, was a White House aide. The playwright, Robert E. Sherwood, did not join the group until the summer of 1940, to work on campaign speeches.

[Kennebunkport]
Nov. 15—'44

Dear Dr. Panofsky:

So there you are and here am I, as we had previously divined; and I think you're wise and right as a cosmopolitan European while I remain a stubbornly determined American Midlander. (You'll have observed that my native sector is Republican, except Mr. McCormick's city of Chicago!) However, to clear things up there are two "points" and the first is your primary reason: the effect on Germany. Of course you're right—a Dewey victory *would* have encouraged Hitler. *We* hold that this would have been very temporary ("lesser evil" etc.) and also that his ensuing *dis*couragement, upon finding the war upon him *intensified* (as it would be in either event), would perhaps *sooner* bring him to ground. He'd come down faster and farther for having gone up. I'm not putting this neatly, I fear; but you'll "get" it, and see the choice of prophetic opinions. *Now*, we who held the other most devoutly hope that the a-type discouragement (Roosevelt's victory in the election) will be effective and sufficient since the b-type can't happen. About a defeated Administration's not being able to conduct negotiations with authority, our feeling is that F. D. R.

would have seen the necessity for Dewey to "sit in."
(F. D. R. declined to "sit in" with poor Hoover in
the emergency of '32—partisan and personal motives
—but he'd accept the reversed position now.)

That's the first "point" and you've probably not
needed this explanation of it. The second is about
the Roosevelt "Master" speech. I'm not sure that he
(precisely) spoke the words printed or that he didn't
and of course there's the process of the whole thing
to consider—Michelson writing the F. D. R.
speeches at that time as R. Sherwood later and at
present, I mean. My memory of the "Master" phras-
ing is doubtless incorrect, as you point out; but I
think it's only too right about the emotional meaning.
He meant Big Business (that is, certain men) and the
unquestionable Michelson (or Corcoran) phrases
"Princes of Privilege," "Economic Royalists" strongly
confirm that intention. His whole *play* at Labor and
the "Underprivileged" is: "I am your champion against
the Rich; *hate* them!" When he said "Master" he
meant the class of people who *were* the "forces" and
congratulated the "underprivileged" upon the power
of their loved Leader.

That's all except some mere discursiveness. You
see an inevitable pattern that means a middle course
for salvation's sake and I don't believe the pattern is
there! or that the New Deal's a solution if it *were*
there!! Our two letters cover all that, and what if
they do? Or if they don't? I take it that neither of us
tries to convince the other; and is any man the less
for having "his own good reasons"—for anything?

Continuing the discursiveness, I mention that
Francis Noble cast the first Republican vote of his life
on November 7 and returned to the "Floats" quite
certain that this settled everything: Dewey was elected.
My own version of what's *certain* is that the "independ-

ent vote" contributed; but that can be said of Hollywood and the Stork Club orators. The decisive elements seem to me: the recipients of Federal "patronage" and salaries; the Solid South (still voting for Jeff Davis) and the C. I. O. and other "labor interests" in Chicago, N. Y. City, Phila., Boston and Detroit. That is, the Solid South and those five cities "swing the country" outside of the huge Administration vote. And a thought by-the-way is that one might ask: Since the South still votes solidly for Jeff Davis (in many sections *against* its own economic interests) for whom and what will the Germans be voting some eighty years hence?

F. D. R. "personally" (discursing on) is a most interesting being. An intelligent cousin of his said, in '32: "I'd rather have him for a cousin or a friend than almost anybody; but I wouldn't vote for him to be *anything*—not even a village constable." You feel that he has humor; I think he has only laughter. "Tommy the Cork," "Henry the Morgue" etc., and roaring over these sallies of his himself. [Alexander] Woollcott, a New Deal and Hyde Park devotee, said, "Brittle— too much like an actor." I have a letter F. D. R. wrote me some years ago—I think it's still in our house in Indianapolis and I'll try to find it (I mean, of course, Betty will) and send you a copy. It's most agreeable, but there's a revelation of infantile vanity that's beyond the singular. A cool-minded Harvard classmate of his described him to me, years ago: "An undergraduate politician," and I've heard that when he was in the Navy Dept. he was "the best poker-player in Washington." And Dorothy Thompson cries, "I love that face!" not meaning his "poker face." Finally we know his indomitable physical courage and that *since* he *dared*, he's been all anyone could ask in regard to Germany. I *hope* he'll eventually be as sound about Permanent Peace, but there again I'm a-tremble.

Betty'll communicate to beg you to let us see you
at Cleeve Gate—we needn't "talk politics" there and
won't have time for it anyhow.

> All our best to you both,
> Faithfully yours,
> Booth Tarkington

*The Trotters of Cleeve Gate would have enjoyed
everything in Panofsky's account of his visit with
them except the misidentification of their six
dogs. They were West Highland White Terriers,
not Sealyhams. Gilmore was Tarkington's butler, a dignified man who was always conscious
of working for a famous author.*

> Princeton, N. J.
> December 4, 1944

Dear Mr. Tarkington,

This is, primarily, to thank you once more for
some other hours "inscribed in gold on scroll of
memory," to quote from Charlie Chan; secondly, to
report that my good wife is, technically, on her feet
since yesterday after our nice young doctor had told
her that she could prolong her life by 6 to 8 years if
she were to stay in bed forever, but that—since this
would not be much fun—she might just as well get up
and "take care of herself" (which is the one and only
thing she will not do; but even so . . .). In addition,
I want to give you the title of that book on Scorel
of which I remembered the author but not the language
in which it is written. Fortunately the language is
French, and the title reads: G. J. Hoogewerff, *Jan
van Scorel, Peintre de la Renaissance Hollandaise*,
The Hague, 1923. This is, so far as I know, the only
full-dress monograph on him, and quite good; more

specialized references are in the book itself and also in Thieme-Becker's *Künstlerlexikon.*

The few hours at Cleevegate were so full of major interests, especially your wonderful gondola story, that I could not report on my little moment of triumph in the taxi that brought me there. The driver had asked me at the station if I would mind sharing the cab with two ladies. They turned out to be a youngish resident of Chestnut Hill* who had met her mother from Westchester, and both, after having cast a fleeting glance upon myself and my fish net (later to be filled with so many inestimable gifts), were naturally extremely contemptuous, not acknowledging my incongruous presence in any way and crushing me further by asking the driver about the estate of Mrs. Stotesbury. But then the car swerved into the driveway of Cleevegate and stopped for the performance of the Ceremony of the Gates: driver dismounting, opening gates; driving on 20 feet; dismounting and closing same. This, I felt, was my chance. Like most attributes (such as the snake, symbol of lewdness as well as prudence) a fish net carries ambivalent implications. It may be, as it was, the attribute of a humble visitor with a fish net. But it may also be the attribute of a country gentleman who does not care. So, while the driver was out for the second time, I said, as negligently as I could: "That's on account of the four Sealyhams." The results were positively amazing. In the few remaining seconds the ladies fell all over themselves with flattering remarks about the house, the gates, the character of Sealyhams, and the view. But I said only that the view was nice as views went, disappeared into the house, and left it to the driver to disillusion the ladies. May

---

* But of fairly recent vintage, I should say.

Betty forgive me for this brief imposture; all done without the "lie direct," merely by sly innuendo.

Yesterday, with Dora fortunately out of bed for the first time, the Burrages came in on their way from Atlantic City where they plan to transfer their activities for the rest of the war. They were absolutely on the top of their form. The first hour and a half was devoted to the saga of the Ration Board, amplified by Mildred's inimitably *Tristram Shandy*-like flashbacks into the histories of about twelve different local and regional characters, and punctuated by the less vocal but all the more impressive prestidigitations of Bob who accumulated before herself an enormous pile of metal objects (in part very, very handsome) previously concealed on and about her person, while briefly supporting or contradicting Mildred's statements with clipped remarks. Near the end of the first half hour, our friend Rensselaer Lee, Editor-in-Chief of the College Art Association, came in with a manuscript of four volumes which he had planned to discuss with me. I gave him a glass of Vermouth, and for the remaining hour he stood before the fireplace, his unemptied glass in his left hand, his four volumes of manuscript in his right, wide-eyed and speechless like a child on his first visit to the circus. Then we had lunch and stayed together for another hour—this second act comprising the no less exciting story of your piano. This story, it would seem, still lacks its final dénouement, and you will doubtless hear more about it directly.

But I perceive that I am about to out-Mildred Mildred, and this in writing. So I hasten to conclude with all our best wishes for yourself, Mrs. Tarkington, Betty, Figaro, and Gilmore.

Yours as ever devotedly,
Erwin Panofsky

*The stained-glass windows in the Tarkingtons'
Indianapolis house may have been brought from
Europe and needed expert knowledge for identification. By "Dr. Frankel," Tarkington meant
Paul Frankl, a colleague of Panofsky at the Institute for Advanced Study who had published
several works on Gothic stained glass. Like
Frankl, Hanns Swarzenski was born in Germany
and emigrated to the United States. He was until
recently Curator of the Department of Decora-
tive Arts and Sculpture, Boston Museum of Fine
Arts.*

4270 N. Meridian Street
[Indianapolis, Indiana]
Jan. 10—'45

Dear Dr. Panofsky:

Thank you for showing the photographs of our
windows to Dr. Frankel; and I'm enclosing a copy
(don't return it) of what Dr. Swarzenski says of the
glass itself. He writes most generously and cordially
in response to my approach and we could hope to see
him someday in Kennebunkport, which is known
to him already, Abris Silberman says. He seems to cover
the doubt inspired by the "frames"—that part of "The
Flight into Egypt" particularly is obviously patched—
and Betty has begun some digging in borrowed books.

When you have a moment do let us have a word
about Mrs. Panofsky's medical new advice—if she has
been taking the treatment and to what effect. We are
impatient to have her as wholly well as she *should*
be. I have a fear that she's too young to take care of herself as people of *my* age take care of *them*selves. *We
learn to be meltable and freezable old wax dolls,
full of much-injured sawdust that may exude, and
collapse us upon the slightest shaking, so we wrap*

cotton-wool about us, move with every cowardly precaution and drowse the hours away. That's not a congenial process for youth or for younger middle-age; but I wish Mrs. Panofsky could adapt herself to at least a part of it.

We greatly enjoyed your account of your arrival at Cleeve Gate and progress thereto. Mrs. Trotter is now constructing a new dog-fence—not *another* so that of gates there would be three, but a fresh one to take the place of the old. In this connection I mention the strangeness of Figaro. We thought we knew him. What a delusion in so fluid a universe! Now, in his eleventh year, he shows a wholly novel and quite alarming sequence of emotions, depths of strange feeling never before even suspected in him. He does not bay the moon; but morning after morning, in bright morning sunshine, he sits and howls with a sonorous resonance that fills the house. He's doing it at this moment, in fact, in such a manner and in such volume as makes it difficult for me to continue this writing, and, I fear, will spoil my enjoyment of any passages interpreted by the French Horn in the next of Dr. Sevitsky's concerts. This French Horn, by the way, called on us the other day and is not French but Russian; and, having been in the United States a mere twenty years, speaks no English. He could, however, drink coffee in any language, so everything passed off well.

Our latest news of Kennebunkport was all of the new hurricane and the Big Tide that covered even the wooden front yard of The Floats, so that Frank Atkins could arrive by the top of the fence only. He will be telling us more—much, much more—next summer.

Faithfully,
Booth Tarkington

Image of Josephine (1945) is laid implicitly in Indianapolis and focuses on Josephine Oaklin, the testy granddaughter of a midwestern millionaire, who lives in a house attached to the museum her grandfather gave to the city. Indianapolis residents wondered how closely Tarkington, as an elderly trustee of the John Herron Art Institute, had based his story on the real squabbles they were having over modern art, especially with the museum's chief patroness. The character John Constable Horne comes perilously close to speaking the author's own mind. Tarkington had no more patience than Panofsky had with abstract art.

The novel sold over half a million copies, but not on the strength of the review in the New York Times *(February 25). After praising* Alice Adams *and* The Turmoil *as Tarkington "at his very best," William Du Bois called* Image of Josephine *"an empty failure," built on a plot "that simply won't wash." "Each character," he continued, "is neatly sandpapered, each scene is milked dry. But this time the novelist's celebrated low comedy reads oddly like vaudeville performed for its own sake." What is more, he found Josephine "as dull as she is cruel." The Panofskys reviewed the reviewer in their letter to Kennebunkport the next day.*

97 Battle Road
Princeton, New Jersey
February 26, 1945

Dear Mr. Tarkington,

it seems impossible ever to be out of debts if one has the privilege of being counted among your friends. I was just sitting down to thank you for your last letter

when the postman rang and brought, simultaneously,
the box of cigarettes and the *Image of Josephine*.
Dora and I spent some time in discussing which of
these three precious gifts we should value most highly.
But finally we decided that, even in this day and age,
the letter should outrank the cigarettes, and that
Josephine should outrank both. *Practical* altruism—
especially when applied to cigarettes in February
1945—is rare enough. But the altruism of the spirit,
as manifested in your letter, is still rarer. It is said,
and generally confirmed by experience, that people
over seventy become "self-centered" and lose some of
the faculty of sympathizing with their fellow-beings,
especially where physical ailments are concerned. But
you have gone to so much trouble to find out about
surgeons and blood pressure and hospitals that no
father or brother could have done more. We are very
much touched, and very grateful. And what shall we
say about the book? It brings back those unforgettable
evenings when it was read to us (on the last evening
we could hardly speak on our way home) and thereby—
in view of the very fact that you allowed us to listen
—seems to have become a tangible and imperishable
symbol of your friendship. And it is a *great* book.
We were so excited in actually holding it in our hands
that we could not bring ourselves to re-reading it *in
toto*; but we opened it here and there, and every passage
seemed to contain the essence of the whole. We think
it is just because of its being so *different* from your
previous books that many people will find it difficult
to evaluate. As an art-historian, I should say it has the
peculiar qualities of the *late* style of great masters—a
style which has one more dimension than that of their
"classic" or middle phase, and has almost invariably
led to a basic misunderstanding, or, rather, non-under-
standing on the part of the contemporaries who simply
could not get over the fact that a *late* Rembrandt did

not show the "golden chiaroscuro" and the definable forms they had so much enjoyed in the middle-period ones, or that there did not seem to be any "tunes" in Beethoven's late quartets. But this applies, of course, to a *comparatively* respectable part of the public, that is, to those who, though bewildered, at least perceive the facts. A creature such as the "reviewer" of your book in the *Times*, which you may or may not have seen (I wish you have not, but I suppose you have) is much worse: he simply does not read the book in the first place; does, therefore, not even *perceive* the facts; concludes, *a priori*, that it is merely a variation on other books by you which he dimly remembers; and finally decides to disapprove, not of what you have written but of what he imagines you would have written if your mind were operating on the same level as his. We know that such things cannot touch you, and that there is such a thing as a judgment of history. But it is an open scandal that such things are possible. You have gone out of your way, in the wonderful chapter XXVI, to give a very direct clue to Josephine's character in the analysis of her "early history" by J. C. Horne—an analysis which, coming from *him*, should settle the matter for any not quite careless reader (the two dry words "Fine Girl," coming from this source, have always struck me as what the Middle Ages used to call a *titulus*). And then such an illiterate person dares to reverse the whole idea—and to criticize the reversal. Every dentist, after all, has to pass some sort of examination before he is let loose on the public, and even the salesgirls at Macy's have to prove that they can read. But in the field of book reviews, at least in the field of "fiction," there seem to be no prerequisites at all. Jean Paul once wrote a wise paragraph expressing his sympathy with proofreaders. They can never really enjoy their reading, he says; for, if they were to pay attention to the meaning of the author, they

Booth Tarkington in front of "Seawood"

Erwin Panofsky and Moses

Booth Tarkington, Figaro, and Peter

Kennebunk River, Kennebunkport, Maine

Photograph by Patrick W. Gra

would overlook all the typographical errors. So
they have always to stick to the words without ever
grasping what they mean, "like a reviewer." But our
reviewers of today don't even respect the words.

Forgive me for being longwinded and violent. But
we were really outraged (not only because of our
admiration for your book but also because of the
principle of the thing), and Dora was—I am not exag-
gerating—entirely put out for an hour because she
was just boiling with rage. Once more, I know such
things do not affect you; but you must allow your
younger friends to be furious.

With all good wishes, and more sincerely gratefully
than words can say,   Yours,
                      Dora & Erwin Panofsky

*In 1933, Tarkington received a gold medal from
the National Institute of Arts and Letters for his
contributions to American fiction. Only William Dean Howells and Edith Wharton had
been earlier recipients. In 1945, he was given the
William Dean Howells medal by the American
Academy of Arts and Letters, an award made
every five years.*

                                March 8—'45
                                Indianapolis
Dear Dr. Panofsky:
    . . . Betty read me what you felt about the N. Y.
Times reviewer and I enclose, as counter-irritant, a
letter just received from a Master John Dell of
Alliance, Ohio. He, as you see, regards me as "one
of the greatest writers in the history of our country"
and he looks upon my power to make him feel "there"

as a "great achievement among writers." The journalistic reviewer declined to share this impression—perhaps because *he* didn't want an autograph—and the best one can hope is that he enjoyed his review. Artur Rubinstein and I were vis-à-vis at dinner the other night and one of the lively things he said was that the audience creates its own concert—all he can do is to give it the opportunity. To any reader a book is what he brings to it and a long while ago I became inured to what newspaper reviewers, usually hurried and always innocently judgmatical, brought to work of mine. "Image of Josephine" had its rewarding audience last summer, for which it is forever grateful; and the novel seems to be included in an award covering these five years and voted by colleagues—for which Mrs. Tarkington will have to make an acknowledgment May 18; so we shall be at Cleeve Gate a bit earlier this year—and by then *all* the news will be good news. Don't doubt that I'm indeed bounden to you for your generous dislike of the *Times* review; I'm sorry only that it annoyed my kind friends. Perhaps, though, it was even useful as a respite—taking your minds for that long off your anxieties. If so I thank the reviewer, who harms me not and helps my friends. Forward, then, with confident hearts!

Yours with continuous
thanks and devotion,
Booth Tarkington

97 Battle Road
Princeton, New Jersey
March 22, 1945

Dear Mr. Tarkington,

I have just returned from Boston, and the first thing I wish to do is to thank you for your last letter, to add my congratulations on the Howells Medal to Dora's,

and, above all, to tell you once more that, if Dora
has stood the ordeal of those long weeks of suspense
as well as she did, this is largely due to the wonderful
loyalty and kindness of our friends among whom you
and Betty hold the first place. Your letters were like
a kind, steadying hand, and we felt that things could
not go entirely wrong so long as you were with us. The
Phillips House in the Massachusetts General Hospital
is a very nice and "high-class" place—so "high-class,"
in fact, that the taxi drivers, upon being given the
address, call you "Sir." But hospitals are, of course,
not really cheerful localities and always remind me
of Louis XIV's sister-in-law, Elizabeth Charlotte of
the Palatinate, who on one occasion almost perished
by thirst in the presence of thirty-five flunkeys because
the particular flunkey, whose office it was to bring a
glass of water, could not be found while the other
thirty-four were not permitted to do anything against
the rules. . . .

                    Yours as ever devotedly,
                    Erwin Panofsky

                                   [Kennebunkport]
                                   April 12—'45
Dear Dr. Panofsky:
    We are like even the ranks of Tuscany who could
scarce forbear to cheer! Loud Princeton-like yells
wouldn't do until Mrs. Panofsky actually could play
Nancy Lee again—"and there she stands and waves her
hands to me at sea." Your *almost* triumphant letter
arrived just as I was sitting down to write you of the wife
of an old friend of mine here. She had that operation
some years ago and it "did everything," as we say, for
her. I didn't know what had happened; remembered
her as a driven shadow and became aware that people
were speaking of her being at lunches, teas, etc. in

great form—this of late leading me to inquire how come.

How *quickly* the whole sky swept off the temporary sepia from its luminous cerulean! Mrs. Panofsky *through* the ordeal—and the lovely house in the village awaiting you! Heaven and all the saints bless the Burrages! So they devote themselves to the war-sick as before—and of course they *do* need just what you'll give to their cherished place. You can be certain the benefit is mutual.

I'm rushing this off to ask you to ask Mrs. Panofsky to try to remember with *pleasure* that Betty'll have coffee for her at the "Floats," where the tide'll be running and the gulls wheeling, just a *few* weeks from today.

Yours in jubilation,
Booth Tarkington

Post-war military problems, the organizing of the United Nations at the San Francisco conference, preparations for Princeton University's bicentennial celebrations, Dora Panofsky's health, and Kennebunkport gossip jostle each other as subjects in these June, 1945, letters.

Frank Aydelotte was Director of the Institute for Advanced Study from 1939 to 1947. Jean Labatut came to Princeton University as Professor of Architecture in 1928. Silas Perkins, eldest son of Captain Fordyce Perkins, was a local Kennebunkport poet who also owned the family coal business. Margaret Deland of Boston was a prolific novelist and short-story writer who used her native Pennsylvania for the background of serious social studies: John Ward, Preacher *(1888),* Philip and His Wife *(1894),* The Iron Woman *(1911),* The Rising Tide *(1916) and others. She and her husband were summer residents long before the Tarkingtons came to Kennebunkport.*

Dear Dr. Panofsky:

"Dora is better!" This from Betty, announced to Mrs. Tarkington and me, was Mozart "making gigue." Once better—after what she went through—means a real *turn*, a decisive swing to the ascent, and must be the *Answer*. I know something of this; my eye got "better" after being out. These betterments make quite a difference.

Our present November weather reconciles us to your not being here immediately; but the B[urrage]'s are making ready for you and in a fury of energy in their accustomed manner. Where they work seems the precise center of the Power House—loud whizzing sounds cease not to be heard from there.

I was delighted, the other day, to have a letter from Mr. Aydelotte on peacetime conscription. I think that all the reasoning and reasonable people oppose it; but fear that this, even of itself, means a minority. Speaking of Princeton, I add that a talk with Prof. Labatut at Chestnut Hill lifted a heavy fog from my hair: I'd undertaken to do the writing for the 200th Anniv. Pageant and couldn't think of *anything*. He, being from the South of France, flashed upon me like a rainbow suddenly sprung over a dismal marsh—I wish he had command in San Francisco.

Came across a friend in reading Sharon Turner's Middle Ages—London, 1825—the other evening: your loved associate. Reference to Suger, his having written the life of Louis le Gros. It was like the glimpse of one familiar and amiable face in a strange, frowning crowd.

News of Kennebunkport: Sile Perkins, after burning down his house by means of an indiscreet grass-fire, has taken his family to live with his sister. Chick is repetitively interested in the rumor that Mrs. Deland left her chauffeur $10,000, and Marian Grandeman has a very altering hairdo, about which there might be real argument.

Faithfully yours,

N. B. T.

"Mr. Rumbin's Blessed Misfortune" is the short story Tarkington built around the objet d'art Panofsky suggested back in November, 1944. Not only did he utilize the gondola of St. Eloy but he also created a character named Professor Schnö-der as the authority on Suger who attests to the objet's provenance. In an article called "The Story of Mr. Rumbin's Gondola" (Inside Information from the Saturday Evening Post, *May 18, 1945), Tarkington gave full credit to Panof-sky for his assistance. The short story appeared in the May 19 issue of the magazine.*

A yearning for "the coolness of Maine" prompted Panofsky to include a footnote in a letter to Betty Trotter on June 22. "Einstein," he writes, "has an old German Encyclopedia in which Princeton is described as a village in the State of New Jersey and seat of a College 'estab-lished there in spite of the fact that the climate is unsuitable for human settlement.' "

Dear Mr. Tarkington,

I have to apologize for being so late in thanking you for your last letter, the date of which I am ashamed to quote, and for the much too generous credit you gave to me in *Inside Information*. But when your letter arrived Dora was unfortunately in rather bad shape. She had contracted a kind of intestinal grip[pe] which superimposed itself upon her recovery, and had to go to the hospital here where she still is. . . . There is still no way of telling *when* we shall be able to travel. We both yearn for the coolness of Maine and the presence of our friends!

In the meantime I am re-writing Suger in galley proof and have made some quite nice additional little "discoveries," including even the name *and portrait* (though in a very clumsy copy of the 17th century which I found, by sheer accident, in Mabillon's *Annales Ordinis S. Benedicti*) of the man who gave the doors of, and probably built, the pre-Sugerian Carolingian Abbey Church. He can be identified by virtue of his having fallen off the scaffold and yet having been saved by courtesy of St. Denis. Perhaps he, St. Denis, may do a similar thing for Dora. I know, one cannot *always* be lucky, and on the whole Dora and I have had a very and, all things considered, miraculously happy life. Only, if there is some power like the classical Nemesis, exacting retribution for too good a time, I wish this power would stick to me instead of poor Dora. In one case Nemesis was really kind. I wonder if you have read of the death of Ernst Cassirer, formerly Professor of Philosophy—and, what is more, philosopher—in Hamburg, then in Oxford, Göteborg in Sweden, Yale and Columbia, and one of our closest friends. He had been giving the last lecture of the term, had lunched with his colleagues, played a game of chess and stood in the entrance of the Faculty Club waiting for a taxi. One of his students happened to see him and offered to wait with him. Suddenly Cassirer gently swayed over, was sustained by the student and died in the student's arms within ten seconds. If it had happened in Rome or Athens it would now be read in Valerius Maximus or Diogenes Laertius.

As a little souvenir in connection with the "Gondola" I am enclosing an authentic portrait—the only one surviving—of our mutual friend [Suger].

With all good wishes,
as ever devotedly yours,
Erwin Panofsky

[Kennebunkport]
June 16—'45

Dear Dr. Panofsky:

What a shocking time for both of you! We, however, hold determinedly to the belief that this attack is, as you say to Betty, one of the vicissitudes of *recovery*. Me, I've had 'em and recall how alarming and painful they can be—especially when the patient has begun to feel that improvement marches. Long convalescences from violences to the system are a series of adventures; they're almost like learning to walk the tight-rope and all movements suggest peril.

What we, here, *expect* is that you'll have easier going after this apparently gratuitous setback and that you'll be in Kennebunkport "almost before you know it" and that Mrs. Panofsky will feel herself in the midst of a miracle, able to travel much more easily than either of you could now anticipate. You've *had* all the miseries of this remedy; you *must* presently have

its other aspects, the blessings. The Burrages, after
a whirlwind of Burragian activity, preparing the
house, have left it ready.

Thank you for the likeness of the great Abbot
who, most suggestively, seems preparing to throw himself through a curling wave and without trepidation.
I see you following that example and Mrs. Panofsky
watching on the beach *long* before the middle of July!

Aff'ly,

N. B. T.

97 Battle Road

Princeton, N. J.

June 22, 1945

Dear Mr. Tarkington,

owing to the vagaries of the Princeton Post Office,
which deposits my mail partly in my house, partly in
the Institute for Advanced Study, partly in McCormick
Hall, and, since June 1, partly in the apartment of
my son Hans, I received your last letter just when I
had written to Betty; the Post Office had left it in
McCormick Hall where I had not been for three or
four days. Since Betty has probably told you "the
news," nothing is left to me but to repeat to you, personally, what you will have heard from Betty: that
you were right, as you always are. Dora's setback,
which sent her to the hospital for a week, was really
nothing but a "vicissitude of recovery." As soon as we
got her home she began to pick up. In fact, the very
contrast between a place where she is at the mercy of
nurses and a place where everybody, including the
undersigned, is at the mercy of her, made her feel
better at once; she stood the heat remarkably well
(perhaps, or at least we love to think so, a first beneficial
result of the operation); could dispense with dope

80   altogether; and today triumphantly negotiated seven steps as a prelude to her new up-stairs life (what a symbol!) in the Palazzo Borraggio. For, we do hope that Bob and Mildred will not object to the unexpected duplication of our domestic staff about which I reported to Betty. So, barring unforeseen contretemps, we are now set for the great adventure, adding the practice of the Virtue of Hope to that of the Virtue of Patience (and thus being two-sevenths righteous, so to speak). The rest is in the hands of God, the Holy Martyrs, and the Pennsylvania Railroad. Once more our gratitude goes out to you for this last link in that chain of wonderful letters which, like the Pseudo-Areopagite's *catena aurea*, "draws us upwards while we, holding onto it with hands raised in alternation, believe to draw it down to ourselves."

Devotedly yours,
Erwin Panofsky

On August 6, 1945, the United States Air Force dropped the first atomic bomb on Hiroshima, Japan. Six days later in Washington, D. C., the "Manhattan District," U. S. Corps of Engineers (the name given by the War Department to the Atomic Bomb Project) released a report on "the development of methods of using atomic energy for military purposes," written at the request of the Director, Major General Leslie R. Groves, by Henry DeWolf Smyth, Chairman of the Department of Physics, Princeton University, and consultant to the Project. In September, Princeton University Press undertook as a public service a reset edition of the government's lithoprint report and published it under the title ber it was in its fifth printing.

For the next five months, atomic energy was, not surprisingly, a constant subject in these letters that passed between Princeton and Kennebunkport. Wolfgang Panofsky had been working in the radiation laboratories of the University of California and had participated in the first nuclear explosion at White Sands, New Mexico; his father knew many of the physicists at the Institute for Advanced Study. Tarkington had written a letter to the Republicans of Indiana as early as May, 1944, urging them to "abandon all taint of isolationism" and to heed this warning, a remarkable statement considering the date: " 'When the next war comes,' all of the military powers concerned will almost certainly be in possession of an implement able to wipe out such a city as New York within ten minutes so effectively that no living being could get anywhere near the place during the next three or four months."

97 Battle Road
Princeton, New Jersey
September 20, 1945

Dear Mr. Tarkington,

I have waited a few days with a direct announcement of our undamaged return (and with our renewed thanks for another beautiful summer in Kennebunkport, made almost perfect by your miraculous influence on Dora's recovery) because I was collecting information as to the estimated time it would take other nations to develop an atomic bomb of their own, given the knowledge now accessible to the general public and a group of competent though not superhumanly brilliant physicists.

The consensus seems to be that it would take the Russians about *three* years (possibly less if they were to work hard and with no regard to waste of labor and materials), and smaller nations such as the French five or six; whereby there is a definite possibility that these hypothetical foreign teams, if they were to work independently of *our* "secret methods," might hit upon something much more devastating than our own bomb which, for the time being, exploits only 1/1000 of the energy theoretically available. Remote though this possibility appears to be, it has to be reckoned with according to the experts (whose view is shared by Dr. Aydelotte, by the way), and this is one more reason for stabilizing the bomb *as is* on an international level rather than embarking upon an atomic armament race with the world at large. I hear that the atomic experts are preparing an official statement to this effect, and I am told that the reasonable view—viz., *your* view, my view, Aydelotte's view, and the view of practically every sane person I have met thus far—is shared by all, quite regardless of party affiliations or convictions as to social and economical problems: the experts comprise Republicans, Democrats, Communists, and what not—yet everybody seems to agree on the essential question, and one young physicist whom I met yesterday after his return from Los Alamos in New Mexico (after having stayed there 2½ years) said, very nicely, that one's attitude toward the international implications of the atomic developments was "simply a test of intelligence."

It is all the more discouraging that this intelligence does not seem to prevail on what is officially known as the "secretarial level." In today's *Times* there is a statement of Undersecretary of War McCloy, literally reading: "The atomic bomb has not removed the need for universal military training but rather intensified the need for such training"; while, *in the same issue,* General Groves, the military director of the atomic project, is quoted as saying that "there is no conceivable defense at present against the atomic bomb" because even the heaviest shelters would afford "only some slight protection" and "not suffice to save a city."

Taking together such contradistinctions with permanent anti-Russian propaganda in our press, with the abolition of the "Denazification program" of Germany (so that we may look forward to millions of nazified veterans instead of to a denazified Germany), one cannot help feeling that some quarters would like to precipitate a "showdown" with Russia *before* those hypothetical "three years" are over and we have lost our temporary monopoly on the atomic bomb.

The bomb, incidentally, has hit Suger, among other things: the Princeton Press prints untold numbers of the Smyth report and had to shelve everything else for the time being. However, since the world has waited 801 years for a translation, it can just as well wait some more—unless the whole question becomes irrelevant in view of further developments in the atomic field. Yet life goes on, playfully as always, and Princeton girds itself for a perfectly unprecedented bicentenary which will not be limited, as I had supposed, to a week of ecstatic celebration but will extend over a period of about 9 months, climaxed by the opening of the New Library and, presumably, the collective funeral of the entire Faculty. The New Library, plans of which we were shown day-before-yesterday, will be very amusing. Like an iceberg, it will be 4/5 underground so that the visible portion, in spite of a tower and a kind of minaret, will not impinge upon the spiritual and architectural supremacy of the Chapel:

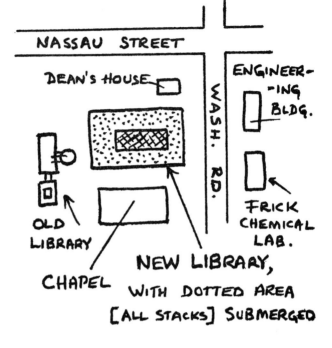

NASSAU STREET

DEAN'S HOUSE

ENGINEER-ING BLDG.

WASH. RD.

OLD LIBRARY

FRICK CHEMICAL LAB.

CHAPEL

NEW LIBRARY, WITH DOTTED AREA [ALL STACKS] SUBMERGED

The emerging part will contain reading-rooms, offices, seminars, lounges, etc., but the subterraneous stacks will be honeycombed with cubicles where one can establish oneself with a temporary accumulation of books, with vertical traffic afforded by automatic elevators and horizontal traffic (this is *my* amendment) by surplus jeeps. Let us hope that this description will induce you to change your intention not to participate in person!

With more thanks than words can convey, and all good wishes from both of us,

ever devotedly yours,
Erwin Panofsky

Dear Dr. Panofsky: Sept. 24, '45

... Suger would be interested to learn of his postponement by the Smyth Report. He might wonder how
much time he'd need in order to become a "nuclear
physicist" himself, for the better protection of St. Denis;
but I'm sure he'd have been up to it and would have
set forth his motive—and his completed atomism, too—
as pious tribute to the proper Sacred Personages.
Whatever he'd have done about it, though, I'm resenting the postponement. Before this earth becomes a
Nova we're entitled to all the pleasure and enlighten-
ment we can get out of it.

Thank you again for placing the New Library
for me and for the description of its subterranean
proclivities. The vertical burrowing seems most
appropriate to these New Times, affording opportunity
for the emergence, some day, of a preoccupied scholar
who may observe with some perplexity the remaining
of nothing at all upon the horizontal plane. He would
at least have the advantage of a Peacetime Conscription
Army.

Nothing of primary importance has happened here
since you left. The event of our summer was, of course,
the magnificent courage with which Mrs. Panofsky
made her recovery. Please give her our devotedly
best wishes, and I hope she has been entertained by
an account, from the Grandemans, of the doings of
the "pre-adolescents" named, by Mr. Fisher, the "Little
Devils' Club." His excitement was caused by some
amusements of theirs—one was soaking tennis balls
in "lighter fluid," setting them ablaze, and rolling them
over the club house floor. Thus perished the ping
pong table etc.

I hope Prof. Labatut is working hard!

Aff'ly,

Booth Tarkington

Charles G. Dawes earned his Army rank as chief purchasing agent for the American Expeditionary Forces in World War I. Under President Harding he served as first Director of the Bureau of the Budget. He was elected Vice President on the Republican ticket with Calvin Coolidge, shared the Nobel Peace Prize in 1925, became Ambassador to Great Britain and later President of the Reconstruction Finance Corporation in the Hoover administration. Tarkington's article, appropriately titled "What a Man!," appeared in Finance *(Chicago) on August 25, 1945.*

Panofsky's bi-lingual pun is literally translated "Maine, which is from madness." If residents of the moon can be called lunatics, then residents of Maine might be called maniacs.

97 Battle Road
Princeton, New Jersey
October 3, 1945

Dear Mr. Tarkington,

your last letter gave us the welcome assurance that all is well on the Kennebunk River, and your charming article about General Dawes, kindly transmitted to us by Betty, conjured up the memory of one afternoon at the Floats when you briefly recounted the incident in the general context of "Maine, *quod est de μαίνεσθαι.*"

The repeated occurrence of the word "General" (capitalized and lower case) reminds me of an anecdote heard yesterday from one of our physicists: after the test explosion of July 16, when the various witnesses were asked about what they had seen, and everybody waxed lyrical in descriptions of the ball of fire, the colors and the plume of smoke, Major-General Groves, the military chief of the project, is said to have answered: "I saw only three stars." This is, of course, a joke, for the printed statement of the Major-General was the most lyrical of all. But in spite, or because, of this (lyrical Generals are never above suspicion) the man seems to be a danger because he can make, and does make, extremely doubtful public statements whereas the experts are still muzzled by the enforcement of military secrecy.

The most beautiful thing in this respect happened quite shortly when a conference of scientists *and* sociologists, economists etc. had been convoked in Chicago in order to discuss the implications of the Atomic Bomb. When the gentlemen convened it turned out that all the *major* scientists who had planned to participate (Urey, Allison, Compton, Szilard etc.) had been ordered to Washington for another, more "urgent," conference in the War Department so that only the "junior members" could attend! Even so, enough were left to answer such questions as could be answered, and it may interest you to hear some of the things that emerged (freely divulged here by three of my colleagues who participated but, I am afraid, not to be used in print).

First, all the scientists agreed that the very use of the word "secret," let alone the use of the word "formula" (as though the Bomb were a hair-tonic) was grossly misleading and should be prohibited. What is still secret are manufacturing tricks which can be discovered, or duplicated, or even improved, within about 3 years *in toto* (which tallies with my previous information).

Second, no "defense" other than the dispersal of all urban developments is in sight. While it is true that aerial defense has been so vastly improved that our large-scale attacks with normal bombs would have been less and less effective had the war gone on, aerial defense against atomic bombing would have to be 100% effective because even 10 planes in a thousand, if coming through, could obliterate New York. Moreover, there would be transatlantic rockets and two perfectly charming possibilities which had never occurred to me:

a) since atomic wars would, of course, start without previous "declaration," the aggressor could simply buy, or hire, some perfectly harmless-looking commercial planes;

b) the component parts of many bombs could be imported into the country to be attacked in diplomatic pouches (plutonium being perfectly safe in quantities smaller than the "critical size")* and then conveniently planted in many key points, with the assembly-mechanism set for a given day and hour.

Third: The only *real* chance of survival: World Government at once, as proposed in a letter from Einstein read at the Conference.

Fourth: World Government impossible at the present moment according to all sociologists and economists.

Fifth: The only *relative* chance, therefore, international control (although this, again according to the sociologists and economists, might lead to so much friction and mutual distrust and/or evasion that the

---

* This "critical size" business is easy to understand: if, in a given spherical mass of plutonium or U 235, a sufficient number of neutrons escape into space, there will be *no* explosion. They escape through the outer surface of the sphere. Consequently, if the *surface* is large enough in proportion to the *volume*, no explosion. Now, the *volume* of a sphere grows at the ratio of r^3, the surface, however, only at the ratio of r^2. Consequently, the smaller the sphere, the larger its surface in proportion to its volume, and the greater the proportion of neutrons escaping into space.

very safety device might turn into dynamite or, rather, U 235 or plutonium).

Sixth: At least, therefore, national government control of all atomic energy, including uranium mines, lest private gentlemen ship big loads of the stuff to Guatemala (but that leaves us pretty much where we were, apart from the fact that the physicists might, and probably will, tackle the other end of the atomic table and liberate the energy, not by splitting heavy elements but by pepping up light ones, as the sun does).

On the whole, there was a tendency to polarize the whole discussion in the direction of U. S. *versus* Russia; and one scientist, only one, had the courage to say: then, why not attack them right away as long as we have the bomb and they don't? Which, indeed, seems to be the only *logical* alternative to *either* World Government (or at least World Government in the sphere of atomic energy) *or* the whole race's dispersing into hamlets, preferably submersible.

Things being what they are, the outlook seems pretty gloomy, and our chief hope seems to rest in the fact that history often proceeded *against* logic, and that there may be, after all, some Supreme Being outside the material universe (which is, at present, finite almost as in the Middle Ages and has room for such a Supreme Being again). But that friend of ours who got the Nobel Prize last year, wrote us: "Who would have thought that most of us would live long enough to be atomized—*and* strongly ionized." We still wonder whether he meant this afterthought about the ionization (which entails an enormous mobility and radio-activity of our component particles after the fact) as a kind of comfort or as something in the nature of "insult added to injury."

We hope that this lengthy and not very cheerful report may be of some interest to you. We hope, too, that you, Mrs. Tarkington and, very particularly, Betty, are quite well. And we are deeply grateful for having met you all, and spent another summer with you, before being atomized—*and* strongly ionized

As ever devotedly yours,
Dora and Erwin Panofsky

97 Battle Road
Princeton, New Jersey
Dear Mr. Tarkington,   October 6, 1945

By way of postscript I am enclosing a clipping from the N. Y. TIMES, October 5, which seems to be an outcome of the Chicago Conference described to you in my last letter.

With characteristic dishonesty, the item is tucked away on p. 4 and neither listed in the "Summary" on the front page nor referred to in the "Index" on p. 24, in contrast to such important news as "Silhouettes will add tone and beauty to new fashions in furs."

So I don't know whether or not this pronunciamento has come to your attention.

As ever devotedly yours,
Erwin Panofsky

"Notes on the A-bomb" and the Panofskys' "long-distance chauffeur" are seemingly disconnected until we know that the sociable Earl Bibber was Kennebunkport's ambulance driver and under-taker. The novelist Kenneth Roberts, on the other hand, author of Arundel *(1930) and* North-west Passage *(1937), a close friend and neighbor since 1919, was a visitor to "The Floats" with whom Tarkington may well have had serious conversations about the looming atomic arms race.*

Dear Dr. Panofsky:

Thank you indeed for the additional notes on
the A-bomb and in particular for the condolence—
subsequent ionization—which I feel duty-bound to
pass on to your recent long-distance chauffeur, Mr.
Bibber, lest he become careless. Probably some other
items in your list should also go to him; one must not
neglect the practical side of such a matter.

The Boston Herald's London correspondent this
morning cables that Russia has begun to make the
bomb, which complicates the process of "giving" it
to her. Our army and navy, supported by many members of Congress, declare their purpose to adopt it as
one of their weapons. It will be placed in the stockpile
on our plane-carriers and thus help to insure the
friendly behavior, toward us, of other nations.
Washington isn't going to let a few scientists, imprac-
tical fellows who try to worry people about mere
possibilities, dictate to our Military Men and the
Representatives of the People. Whistlers in the dark
emit over and over the tune: "We Always Do Find
Counter Measures." This helps us to think about something else.

The problem seems to begin to clarify itself.
International Control of the bomb for production of
Peace appears to be our alternative to world suicide.
Of course that makes gods of the Board of Control—
they could make the rest of us do anything, and they
may intrigue, split into cliques, develop a dictator-
chairman, heaven knows what; but they are, now
apparently, our best bet. So we'd have to work for it.
How? I can't think of a better way than by using
the daunting truth.

That is, as I've pressed in the bits I've been doing,
the wisdom of fears should be encouraged. The

Dignity of the Common Man needs sufficient impairment to permit him to wobble at the knees. The method must be humble rather than overbearing and without banshee wailing. Scare a guy the wrong way and he'll hate you for it and stop listening—yet he's got to be scared. A judicious frightening of the populace by means of the "plain truth" plainly presented by sharers of the common danger, and to this the added suggestion that there is one way out—Control for Peace. I can't see a better campaign. It will be resisted—Big Wigs, Brass Hats, and those who *can't* see because they can't *take* it, and old-grooved minds too deeply worn down. (Poor old McCormick thinks of the A-bomb only as how it may bear upon his plan to elect MacArthur.)

You and Mrs. Panofsky must be having some interesting hours with your Princeton colleagues— I hope she's *up* to *hours* of them. Here we have only Mr. Noble and Mr. Roberts. Mr. Noble broods upon the A-bomb as an incentive to Gilbert and Sullivan-type plots and choruses. Mr. Roberts has no time for atomic thoughts; his new farm-hand stops work to light cigarettes. Frank Atkins is better material but is more concerned with the portrait the New Orleans lady did of him.

The Burrages loom; we look forward to being dizzified by Thursday. Betty's done an astonishing ¾ view in modeled plastic of a rugged old subject and intends to do next a mask of Mr. Noble for her "Ghastly Corner." He conceals his flatteredness under a mask of his own—affected resistance. Chick whistles and sings (to himself, of course) and so do his fellow-villagers, because everything looks empty again; and Weinstein's prepares to close. Finally, there's quite a prospect that the big "Rogers Estate" across the river will be purchased for use as an Inebriates' Private Asylum and all Natives strongly advocate this measure.

Naturally! The Inebriates would be here all winter
and are a class notoriously and generously interested
in adding to their number. Already many converts
are waiting thirstily.
Our best to you both,
Aff'ly
N. B. T.

*During the last months of 1945, Tarkington
could not seem to take his mind off the subject
of man's survival in the face of the atomic bomb.
Two Indianapolis speeches ("Shall We Choose
Insanity?" and "Let's Look Before We Leap")
had been printed before the end of the war in the
Appendix to the* Congressional Record *(Vol. 91).
His September 9 speech ("Fools Will Burn") was
printed in* The Lutheran Outlook *(November)
and an article called "It's Time To Be Afraid"
appeared in* This Week Magazine *(November
11).*

*What disturbed Panofsky while writing this
letter were three reports in the New York* Times
*(October 14): first, the newly-organized Atomic
Scientists of Chicago were objecting to a statement from the House Naval Affairs Committee
which said "indications" were that "an effective
counter-measure to atomic bombs has been
developed"; second, the Association of Los
Alamos Scientists (Panofsky calls this group "the
bomb experts") were arguing that trying to keep
the invention from the rest of the world would
"lead to an unending war more savage than the
last" and that above all "the use of atomic energy*
must *be controlled by a world authority"; and
third, Chairman Andrew J. May of the House
Military Affairs Committee, after refusing to re-*

open hearings on the May-Johnson Bill to control and nationalize atomic energy, published in support of his action a telegram from J. Robert Oppenheimer, Enrico Fermi, and Ernest C. Lawrence, a political move which distressed Panofsky as much as it must have distressed the three atomic physicists.

97 Battle Road
Princeton, New Jersey
October 14, 1945

Dear Mr. Tarkington,

your last letter was a great comfort in that it shows your firm determination to continue the fight for sanity against all odds. The odds, it seems, are terribly heavy—with the Naval Affairs Committee spreading what everybody moderately familiar with physics *knows* is a plain lie, and practically all the newspapers playing down all opposition to what seems by now to be accepted policy. Still today (Sunday) even the NEW YORK TIMES gave front page space to the brave protest of the bomb experts and also printed, without, however, calling attention to the flagrant contradiction between this statement and the Naval Affairs Committee's, General Groves' unequivocal denial of any effective defense. On the other hand, they printed, directly following the protest of the scientists, Chairman May's dishonest release of a telegram from Oppenheimer, Fermi and Lawrence endorsing the present "nationalization" of atomic laboratories, uranium deposits etc., which, of course, is not at all tantamount to their endorsing the "secrecy" policy. To keep uranium and atomic research out of private speculation does, after all, not mean to "keep it for ourselves." In fact, Oppenheimer, Fermi and

Lawrence expressly stated that they hoped that the
present legislation might be the "first step" to better
things, meaning an international settlement. In reality,
the opinion of the scientists is not 90% but 100%
reasonable. What Mr. May tries to sell as an expression
of dissent has nothing to do with the case; and in this
connection you might be interested in the enclosed
excerpt from a letter from our little [son] Wolf[gang]
who announces that he has now accepted a very nice
and decent offer to do *pure* research in the Radiation
Laboratory at Berkeley University (under Lawrence)
and looks forward to work "without worrying about
the opinion of incompetent brass hats." If this case is
as typical as it would seem to be according to his letter,
there is really a great danger that our silly policy will
lead to a kind of sit-down, or rather walk-out, strike
of the best men in physical research—so that our very
obsession with "security" and "preparedness" will
actually defeat itself by way of a direct cause-and-effect
nexus. The only logical alternative seems to be war
(atomic war) right now, or at least very soon; and if
one reads of plans to ultra-rehabilitate Germany so as
to produce 10 billion tons of steel as against 4.5 in
pre-Hitler days and to live "at least as well" as the
victims one feels inclined to believe that there is, not
so much method in our madness as madness in our
method.

One other comfort in this autumn of our dis-
content—apart from your letter—was an all-too-brief
visit of the Burrages who by now must have reached
Kennebunkport. They cheered us up beyond belief,
and will certainly do the same for you. Dora tells me
that Betty finds our correspondence too atomic lately,
and she has written to her in a less nuclear vein. I am
afraid the ladies are right; but I find it hard—though
it has to be done—to keep my mind off these problems;

which, however, does not diminish my affection for those who are a little fed up with the atom, and for Betty in particular.

With all our warmest wishes and, again, many thanks.

Devotedly yours,
Erwin Panofsky

[Kennebunkport]
Oct. 18, '45

Dear Dr. Panofsky:

Yes—a lot of thick heads have to be relieved of layers of fat before we can have any "proper action" in Washington. Some of the heads there—indeed many rather than "some"—are nothing *but* fat; no use to bother 'em. Truman's a type long fairly familiar to me; you find him in Maine as well as Indiana—in all the States. Democratic politician, nationalistic, "well-meaning," his mind like his vocabulary tied to stencils and inclined to resist enlightenments that require unprecedented perceptions. The *quality* of T's *voice* tells you pretty well what manner of man he is. Yet he can be reasoned with, *has* a perception of *facts*. He cannot avoid his "training"—that is, his experience—which makes him think *first* of the fact's effect on voters. Coolidge was shrewd. I think I told you how he said to a few of us who'd just dined with him: "U.S. Senators vote only as they think will get *them* the most votes back home." Truman was a senator and *had* been a haberdasher—obliging his customers.

There's a kind of "average American" sensibleness about him nevertheless and although one would usually have to persuade the people before he'd think it wise to be persuaded—which is any politician's typical position.

An Indiana friend wrote me lately: "People don't want to think about the A-bomb. This is like their thought of death—it's a grisly thought, therefore to be avoided, and they feel there's no *use* thinking about it because there's nothing they can do about it."

The effort, of course, then, must be to have them see that they *can* do something about the A-bomb; that it *can* be avoided. They at once tend to a side-track: "Maybe all countries can be persuaded to agree never to use A-bombs." That seems to be the prevalent escapist twist—and naturally has no great conviction behind it. Somewhere in the coils of the wriggling mind is a knot—"Maybe a government whose panzer divisions were being driven back might be desperate enough to break the agreement—so what's the use trying to do all this? What's at the movies today?"

Inertia has to be broken up and I can't see a more effective breaker-upper than fear—a hideously war-ranted one—but that emotion needs to be roused adroitly and then managed with care. Otherwise the voter says: "Trying to scare *me*? I'm no simp!" Hates the scarer and puts the shivering out of his mind; votes as usual without stirring up his congressman. . . .

"The Burrages"—it sounds like a sect—have their new furnace *in*, today. In the neighborhood that means "talents of the highest order," as you and Mrs. Panofsky well know. They came for "Floats" coffee, seasoned by Mr. Atkins's thumb, yesterday, and we A-bombed until dusk. Of course they gave us their news of you and I needn't say how happy we were made by their impressions of Mrs. Panofsky's present and future. Hurrah! We all *knew* it!

No further news has come in about the prospect of an Inebriates' Home across the river, I'm sorry to say, except that the prospective purchaser *has* been here. If it happens, the nostalgia for Mr. Noble may become unbearable. Betty had, strangely, a favorable opinion from him of her three-quarter-view head of me, and

I fear it means a softening in his character. Mr. Atkins has supplied the "Floats" with its coffee-sugar from his own stock; but makes Mr. Noble use molasses instead—a stern man, Mr. Atkins! When he disapproves, he shows it.

That is all—except that an unfortunate moose was shot (strictly against the law) at Cape Porpoise and that clammers are digging up the whole backyard of the "Floats," to the audible annoyance of the gulls; and I'm sure it will be no news that we miss the Panofskys more continually than ever.

Aff'ly,
NBT

[Kennebunkport]
Oct. 29—'45

Dear Dr. Panofsky:

My "*completely* pessimistic" English friend writes that he will soon have more to tell me, confidentially, and that this "more" is "not of a kind to allay anxiety." In the meantime I'm wondering what hint you may be able to give me about the *possible* area of destruction under a single explosion and at what height the burst would be effective below. Does the area increase proportionately to the height—and with what probable mitigation? I shoot in the dark as you may have no information on the point; I just want to know all I *can* before reaching Indianapolis. I'm usually interviewed there and the "Com[mittee] for Victory" have asked for another broadcast—so the opportunity seems legitimate. Of course the conscriptionists, the Legion, the Navy League, and the Democratic machine would rather I speak not. Discretion will be my watchword.

I may add that, according to "the Burrages," our village is daily shaken by laughter and some explosions of our gardener's ordering. He needs a drainage ditch for our meadow and is having it prepared by T. N. T. As the bank is in mud, not far below the surface, the noise and concussion are Something! and Mr. Roberts is loud in complaint that his stone house shakes pitiably. The K'port mirth is stimulated by the fact that two years ago his own ditching by this method shook down two ceilings in the village, etc. etc. etc. The B's are in pure delight and thus far we have shattered only two windows—one of our own and one, alas, of Mr. Maling's. Happily he is not here—though I know he'd be forgiving. (The glass of Mrs. Tarkington's hot-house isn't doing at all well.)

Marian Grandeman's in a Portland hospital, having had a rather serious operation; she won't be home, Mary says, for three weeks. However, the recovery, I believe, is assured. At the "Floats" Mr. Atkins has given up his long struggle with the seagulls. We sit in the sun there, nevertheless, when there *is* one, and Betty works on a mask—Mr. Noble in "full face," quite a sight! He is flattered—and yet positive that the result is caricature; it isn't. Our Mr. Chick is in unexampled high spirits and *sings*, somewhat to himself but not altogether, most of the time when he isn't driving. We heard him sing to Fig[ar]o: "It ain't goin' to rain no more."

Aff'ly,
N. B. T.

97 Battle Road
Princeton, New Jersey
October 31, 1945

Dear Mr. Tarkington,

for several days I had a fairly bad conscience because I had not answered your letter of October 18, but in Princeton, in sharp contrast to Kennebunkport, nothing ever happens. Thomas Aquinas made the famous statement: "Nothing is in the mind but what has been in the senses before." And though Leibnitz amended this by adding: "excepting the mind itself," this amendment did not do much good in my case, the "mind itself" being completely blank, owing to the hopeless aspect of the newspapers, on the one hand; the equally hopeless plight of the humanities, on the other; and two whole weeks of final proofreading, on the third, so to speak. Now I am exceedingly ashamed to receive another, again perfectly delightful letter from you, and the only thing I can do is to answer this one by return mail (the German expression is, more dramatically, "postwendend"—one actually sees the old mail coach turning round on its rear wheels and dashing off in the opposite direction). So I got hold of a great physicist at once and laid your questions before him. As always, things are not so simple, and *exact* figures are, of course, either unknown or unmentionable . . . .

On the whole, the scientists have done pretty well in setting up an audible howl, and have at least prevented the May-Johnson Bill from being railroaded through the House without discussion. My informant tells me that the Army *originally* wanted the Bill passed even without being *read* to the House! In the meantime, the great exodus of top-ranking physicists continues because they naturally wish to publish and to read the publications of others (as they already do in neutral countries while the Russians apparently do not publish either but work like beavers). It is, indeed, quite stupid, even *granted*, for argument's sake, the desirability of an atomic armament race, to try to muzzle the scientists *without having the terroristic powers* that would prevent them from simply quitting. The Russians can tell Mr. Kapitza to produce an atomic bomb within a year or be shot at dawn on that date—we can prevent Mr. Oppenheimer or Mr. Urey

from talking or writing about atomic problems, but
we cannot, as yet, prevent them from simply going
off and working on cosmic rays or the morphology
of hoar-frost.

One great physicist here said, as I so often thought,
that our only hope of survival* would be to destroy
Russia within the next two years—but these are things
which just the normal politician, whose redeeming
feature is, after all, the consciousness of his own
limitations in the sight of God, will not easily do.
The *great* crimes can be committed only by people
who *know* that they are *right* in the sight of whatever
God they accept—the devils and the saints. We admire
you more than words can express for your determination to carry on with the good fight.

> With all good wishes,
> Yours as ever devotedly,
> Erwin Panofsky

* unless we choose to be sensible in the eleventh hour

*The archaeologist Peter Heinrich von Blancken-
hagen was a friend of Panofsky both in Hamburg
and at the Institute of Fine Arts, New York University. His report on post-war German politics
may have recalled for Tarkington his own brief
skirmish with entrenched power as a freshman
Representative in 1903 in the Indiana legislature.*

*The lines from Shakespeare are spoken by
Richard Scroop, Archbishop of York, to the opponents of the king in* Henry IV, *Part Two (I,
iii, 89-90). The Archbishop later quotes an English proverb which Tarkington would have well
understood in 1945: "Past and to come seems
best, things present worst."*

*Helen Morrison ran a taxi service in Kenne-
bunkport which, on the day of the Tarkington
family's departure, frequently took the entourage
as far as Mayor Curley's Boston.*

[Kennebunkport]
Nov. 13, '45

Dear Dr. Panofsky:

Thank you indeed for letting me see the extract
from Mr. v. Blanckenhagen's letter. It is enlightening
and I take to myself the benefits therefrom. Nationalistic imperialism has always been the real foe of good-
will, hasn't it? Nazism seems only an acute expression
of that demon, and "Nature" has always employed
what *we* think evil and has used it in a manner that
appears to us as discouragingly offhand. In spite of your
feeling that the American people always recover their
balance, I'm not sure that the Germans ought to be
brought to *our* kind of "real democracy." A true
Republic, yes indeed, if that could be. My slight
practical adventure into politics, of which I fear I too
often and tiresomely speak, implanted a doubt of
democracy's possible existence and of its value, *could*
it live. Favorite quotation, oft repeated:

An habitation giddy and unsure
Hath he that buildeth on the vulgar heart.

The manipulations of our democracy play to that
heart and their habitation is sure so long as they feed
it from the public till and from their store of flattering
platitudes. This *sounds* like bitterness but has the
appearance, to me, of nothing much more sour than
long observation founded on that ancient experience
in a campaign and a session of our Hoosier legislature.
Besides, I didn't hate the politicians, and I still like
them.

I'm glad you're going to the meeting of the Philos[ophical] Society and the Acad[emy] of Sciences; I hope you'll speak there and that you'll spare time to let me know the gist of the expressions. Washington and the Brass Hats have made *too* clear what *ruling* minds are like! Only here and there has been a hint of perceptive imagination, and certainly none of this has come from Truman. On the A-bomb he's been consistently the wrong man's parrot. In time a right man may teach him other words; Atlee may get a few into his echoing vocabulary.

Saturday night we dined with the Burrages and you and Mrs. Panofsky appeared to be with us almost substantially. Yesterday Mrs. Middleton gave a farewell tea to the summer's survivors and Betty reports more than a dozen present gaily. On Thursday our caravan begins to move, with Mrs. Morrison as guide as far as Mr. Curley's recovered oasis. If another Mrs. Morrison is available we might get from Chestnut Hill to Princeton instead of petitioning you to inconvenience yourself again so generously as heretofore. We'll communicate.

With the best from all of us to all of you,
Aff'ly,
N. B. T.

Chestnut Hill
Nov. 29—'45

Dear Dr. Panofsky:

Fiasco of my devising. My plan was to descend on you and Mrs. Panofsky (after brief advance warning) by hired car from here—Mrs. Tarkington, Betty and I—after lunch for perhaps a two-hour sight and sound of you. First I had to clear off some unavoidable appointments which included three different agents (lit and movie), a playwright (dramatizing "Rumbin Galleries"), the Kahlers, who'd written a virtual "must" to Mrs. Tarkington, and a Princeton contemporary on his last legs, a Trustee of the museum here whom I've put off for two years as a guide to the Landsdowne Room. This done and free time found, we'd gallop to Princeton and be doing it just about tomorrow.

In the meantime we grew more and more uncomfortably aware that the station agent here hadn't been able to say *when* he'd have "reservations" for Indianapolis to dispose of. Yesterday he said: "The greatest travel pressure in history is on. I don't know what we can do for you. Keep your trunks packed and be ready to leave the first chance I find for you. You'd better go *then* as the nearer Christmas comes" etc. This morning he has telephoned that he *has* a third of the space we usually feel the need and his strong advice is to *take* it. If we don't, we sit handy to the telephone and with all luggage packed, not daring to go even into town—and for how long he can't say. So we take it and that cuts out the excursion we'd set store by.

We'd felt it would be pretty piggish to ask you to go to the inconvenience of still another trip to Cleeve Gate, and we did hope to see Mrs. Panofsky too—by *our* doing the traveling. My bright little plan didn't allow for post-warness. . . .

I can't tell you how much disappointment for us is involved in the mess the still powerful Hitler has made of my chart. Betty, who's *very* much better, doesn't permit me to meet her eye—the eye of reproach. So I have disgrace to add to disappointment—and a bag full of unanswered questions of a dozen different kinds. Woe's me!

Aff'ly
NBT

Panofsky's concerns in this letter are typical of his expansive imagination coping with the difficulty of putting both large issues and "the little immaterial things" on paper. Some deletions are made only to avoid repetition.

The "new Director" of the Institute, J. Robert Oppenheimer, did not succeed Frank Aydelotte until 1947. He was still chief of the Los Alamos laboratories in 1945 and thus closely associated with such fellow physicists as Eugene Wigner and Enrico Fermi. Major General Leslie R. Groves had supervised the development of the atomic bomb, but in the post-war years he increasingly came into conflict with American scientists. Time described him (February 25, 1946) as "a blustering, tactless, fanatically secretive militarist."

97 Battle Road
Princeton, New Jersey
December 5, 1945

Dear Mr. Tarkington,

We were, of course, very much disappointed when your intention to come to Princeton was frustrated by the traffic manager in Philadelphia—that humble, yet so efficient representative of the Traffic Manager *in excelsis.* But, on the other hand, we were relieved to hear that it was nothing worse. Not knowing that you stopped over in Boston so long, we were very much afraid that you might have caught that grippe which makes the rounds here for several weeks and has got hold of nearly every one in sight (only I myself, like Milton, still "stand and wait"). Praise be that this fear was groundless! The worst part of it is that I shall not be able, much though I should love to, to accept your kind invitation to see you in Indianapolis in

January. My lecture in Cincinnati is so tightly squeezed in between a seminar and a Committee meeting (the latter still more futile as it concerns proposals for our new Director about whom the Trustees have certainly made up their minds for months, yet not to be missed) that I must hurry back and forth with the smallest possible delay. But there will always be a Kennebunkport—let us hope.

I should have loved to report to you on the meeting of the Philosophical Society and the National Academy of Sciences orally rather than in writing; for, the material core of the proceedings was, of course, relatively meagre in comparison with the little immaterial things that are so difficult to "commit to the point of the pen" as Suger loves to put it. On the whole it was very nice. There were so many Nobel prize winners around that one felt positively naked without this closest equivalent of a halo in a godless period, and even the not yet ennobeled scientists, such as Oppenheimer or Wigner, wore the invisible nimbus of atomic mystagogues. Incidentally, a few weeks ago a new Nobel Prize descended upon one of our dearest friends and colleagues here—Mr. [Wolfgang] Pauli, the discoverer of the "neutrino" and the famous "Pauli exclusion principle" by virtue of which a table or ink-pot is just as large as it is—and after a very nice, private celebration in our house (only six or seven people, but Mozart's Coronation Concert[o], providentially available in a quite small record shop in Philadelphia after three years of unsuccessful research) I shall have to propose his health on an official Institute's Dinner with 100 portions of chicken and green peas.

To revert to the Philadelphia Meeting: of course, no more actual facts could be revealed than were known before or became known shortly after through the press reports which you have probably seen:

Oppenheimer—who gave by far the best talk, starting
with the sentence: "We have created an evil thing,"
ending with an almost *verbal* reiteration of your unforgettable formula, "the only imaginable defense is
peace," and finally acclaimed with a spontaneity quite
unexpected in about the stuffiest audience in the
world—ventured the estimate that *cost* of atomic
bombs would shortly be reduced by the factor 1:1000,
and that *our* loss in an atomic war would be about
40,000,000 lives (to which, as you may have read,
General Groves, referred to by the physicists as "The
Idiot," cheerfully replied that the remaining 80,000,000
could still win, provided, that is, that they did not
contract cancer of the bones from radiation about $1\frac{1}{2}$
years afterwards). Oppenheimer is a very fine, cultured
man, enormously rich, interested in horses, Impres-
sionists and mediaeval French, and greeted me
afterwards with the remark that he knew both my
sons very well (a remark repeated by several other
scientists afterwards so that I, *mutatis mutandis*, began
to feel like the Princeton gentleman known only as
"Mrs. Swan's husband"). Fermi gave a talk about
the actual experiments leading up to the production
of plutonium Pu 94^{239} not transcending the Smyth
report but very entertaining owing to Fermi's gesticula-
tive vivacity and almost Rumbinesque language. The
most interesting talks from a factual point-of-view
were those of a (purely negativistic) economist from
Chicago, named [Jacob] Viner, who believed, contrary
to common opinion, that the "next war" would not
begin, but *end* with the use of atomic bombs since
all the powers would *first* try to win *without* suffering
the "Oppenheimer losses" threatening the victor as
well as the loser; and of [Irving] Langmuir, the research
director of General Electric. Langmuir first gave a
very positive picture of scientific life in Russia, where
he had been with a group of scientists also including

some colleagues of mine whose private accounts tally with his: lots of Institutes devoted to purely *theoretical* research (very surprising in a theoretically Marxist set-up), lots of incentives and distinctions for individuals, in sum, as he phrased it, a "system that has incorporated the best features of capitalism while the Western nations tend to incorporate the worst features of communism.". . .

Please forgive me for this long and somewhat rambling letter, and accept our warmest wishes for yourself and all your house.

As always devotedly yours,
Erwin Panofsky

Dec. 9, '45
Indianapolis

Dear Dr. Panofsky:

This makes it a double blow—or triple: no Chestnut Hill, no Princeton, and now no Indianapolis. Down with the Seminar! He has reigned too long. We had confidently expected to bring upon you enough pressure to have you with us at least overnight and were moving several objects of art into obscurities where they would not distress your thoughts; so you comprehend what chagrin is involved in your coming within easy range only to disappear.

We're indeed indebted for your letter on that meeting. It's hair-raising for hair already vertical and I show it confidentially to a few friends, among whom is the partner of a Republican Boss. I'm not able to predict what we may expect from that political party; though once I could have reassured you; it would have been more intelligent than the other and have had better "basic principles." I think that "in a general way" this may still be so; but the long degeneration seems to have changed types—the "typical Republican,"

once an excellent citizen and not unenlightened, is
probably somebody else nowadays. . . .

I suppose you've seen that Mr. Byrnes proposes
to put the A-bomb with the 51 Nations rather than
with the Security Council. For my part, though I've
advocated the Council, I think he may be right. It's
a tricky affair; but the Holders of the bomb mustn't
be subject to a veto and the world *should* be safer if
all of its peoples stand equal before the Law—the law
of the bomb—and are represented on the bench.
Perhaps the Security Council could be made over to
that effect and the veto power be abandoned. I hope
the new Conference will realize that it's time to forget
the Brave New World and stop the 4-Freedoms
oratory. Progress is made through Fear and Self-
Interest, not otherwise, and the only present business
of the world is to try to live, which of course means
to try not to kill—peace being at long last the only
possible policy for all governments including the
predatory. Nature is showing her hand, and, though
Oppenheimer said "We have created an evil thing,"
I think the thing was there, already, waiting to be
unveiled—evil to *us* if we choose to live a little while
longer in our old evil follies. I was delighted to know
that Gen. Groves could be identified simply as "The
Idiot." Brass Hats! They can't let go; and yet, when
we had an infestation of termites in this house, last
year, and the bug-destroyers finished 'em off, it seemed
proper to call in our carpenters. Of course the comparison is imperfect, especially as the destroyers didn't
need to fear that their business was about to become
extinct.

Perhaps I'm putting these scribblings upon you
because I've got to produce another broadcast for our
Indiana Com[mittee] For Victory—a New Year's sort
of thing—and hope that if my notions aren't identical
with yours you'd maybe drop me a line of reinstruction.

It would be much more satisfactory here if some advantageous dislocation should happen to King Seminar and *yet* bring you in person this way. *Should* such a gratifying possibility become actual, an hour's notice to Indianapolis would suffice and your room be waiting.

Mrs. Panofsky understands that it's only your official duties that we're resenting—*not* your immediate return to *her*. Please give her our love and best holiday wishes and tell her that Betty is really "coming round all right" as are we all.

Aff'ly,

N. B. T.

The Pearl Harbor investigations of 1945 had wide repercussions. Major General Patrick Jay Hurley, Ambassador to China for ten months, resigned his post early in December. During the Congressional hearings he charged that career diplomats George Atcheson, Jr. and John S. Service had thwarted him and the official United States policy of supporting General Chiang Kai-shek's Central Government. Secretary of State James F. Byrnes immediately came to the Department's rescue.

97 Battle Road
Princeton, New Jersey
December 15, 1945

Dear Mr. Tarkington,

Your dear letter of December 9th made me very sad because of the disappointment you seem to feel on account of my not being able to come to Indianapolis in January (although this very disappointment made me feel quite proud—such is the human soul—at the

same time). But the letter was, in itself, a rich compensation by the light it throws on the political
problems which I shall never quite understand. Being,
as you know, a convert to the *Herald-Tribune*, I find
myself nearly always in complete agreement with
what they say, even with their extremely decent
attitude to the Pearl Harbor investigation and the
Hurley excitement. And yet it seems that, *within*
the Party, there are so strong contrasts, not only in
private feelings and actions but also in official or semi-
official tendencies, that the outsider, reading the
Herald-Tribune editorials, on the one hand, and
the speeches and queries of the Republican members
of the investigation Committee on Pearl Harbor, on
the other, is simply bewildered. Still, hope never dies,
and the recent developments in the Atomic Bomb
question look a *little* better—though the apparent
change in attitude, even supposing it to be more than
apparent, may easily come too late. Incidentally, I
wanted to call your attention to the fact that Oppenheimer's address to the Philosophical Society has been
reprinted in full in the *Saturday Revue of Literature*,
November 24, p. 9. They ran a special section on
Atomic Problems since Nov. 17, and this was the
second article in this series. It was not mentioned
that it was identical with the Philadelphia speech; so
I wonder whether it has caught your or Betty's eye.
I should have included a clipping, but I don't keep
the *Sat. Rev. of Lit.* myself and, as usual, was quite
unable to secure a copy of that number in the local
stores. I am including, however, a little speech of my
own contrivance, not because I think it remarkable
but because it was given on the occasion of that Nobel
Prize dinner for my friend Wolfgang Pauli about
which I wrote you last time with justifiable trepidation.
It was indeed a very trying task to speak in competition,
as it were, with only [Hermann] Weyl, who spoke for

the mathematicians, and Einstein (the economists were cancelled "on account of fog," as one might have said by way of analogy with the Staten Island Ferry); so I was supposed to furnish some comic relief (but the pun about the "general public" on p. 2 was entirely unpremeditated and occurred to me only when I remembered the "Smyth Report" while I was talking).

In the meantime the great secret of the 200 master-pieces brought to Washington from Berlin has been announced in the daily press, and it is funny to think of Jan van Ecyk's *Virgin in a Church* and Dürer's *Holzschuher* as now being within 200 miles of Princeton but probably invisible. Everybody speculates, of course, what the *real* reasons may be: mortgage against reparations, or obviation of possible claims by the Russians? Not even the "usually well-informed circles" seem to have any idea.

Dora has stood the Nobel Prize dinner very well (the ladies, even in frail health, are always better in living up to this kind of thing than we are) and joins me in kind remembrances, warmest wishes for Christmas and the New Year, and fond hopes for the summer.

As ever devotedly yours,
Erwin Panofsky

This speech was delivered in Fuld Hall, Institute for Advanced Study, Princeton, New Jersey, on December 10, 1945.

To most of us the Pauli Exclusion Principle, for which our guest of honor received the Nobel Prize, is less familiar than his other world-famous achievement, inexcusably omitted from the official citation: the celebrated "Pauli Effect." This, too, is—in a sense

—based upon an "exclusion principle." Wherever
Pauli appears—or, rather, appeared, for the phenomenon has tended to abate somewhat in recent years—
major or minor catastrophes can be observed to happen
to animate and inanimate objects in the vicinity
—*excluding* Pauli himself.

Hundreds of cases in point have been reported
and many of them have been retold in the last few
weeks, for instance: the case of the two dignified
ladies who simultaneously and symmetrically collapsed
with their chairs on either side of Pauli as soon as he
had taken his seat in a lecture hall; or the case of
the railroad train that came apart *en route,* with
Pauli merrily proceeding to his destination in one
of the front cars while the others were left behind.
I will not carry coals to Newcastle but merely add, for
the record, what happened to myself when I first met
the Laureate sixteen or seventeen years ago. The
mutual friend, who had the very good idea of introducing us, had asked us to lunch in a lovely outdoor
restaurant near Hamburg, where luncheon could be
extended until about four o'clock in the afternoon;
then the fortress was taken by superior forces of ladies
armed with knitting bags. When we reluctantly rose
at this point, it turned out that both our host and
myself had been sitting in whipped cream for about
three hours—but not Pauli.

However, all these tales have tended to obscure
a more important and no less mysterious phenomenon
that may be termed the *"Pauli Effect in Reverse."*
The "Pauli Effect Proper" affects physical bodies, and
affects them adversely. The "Pauli Effect in Reverse"
affects minds and souls, and affects them beneficially,
stimulating them, making them more conscious of
themselves, charging them with an induced electric
current, as it were—even if they happen to be the
minds and souls of *humanists.*

On a purely factual plane the humanist can learn but little from his scientific friends. He might want to read what they write; but he would not be able to understand it, unless they charitably condescend to the general public or a public of generals. The scientists, on the other hand, might be quite capable of understanding what the humanist writes; but they would not want to read it.

On a more fundamental—and, at the same time, more human—plane, however, the twain can meet and exchange their experiences. And here the humanist, if he is fortunate enough to find the right mentor, can benefit very much by a discussion. There are, after all, problems so general that they affect *all* human efforts to transform chaos into cosmos, however much these efforts may differ in subject matter. The humanist, too, finds himself faced—once he attempts to *think* about what he is doing—with such questions as: the changing significance of spatial and temporal data within different frames of reference; the delicate relationship between the phenomenon and the "instrument" (which, in the case of the humanist, is represented by the "document"); the continuous and/or discontinuous structure of the processes which we lightheartedly call "historical evolution."

In matters like these the humanist can and does receive help from the scientist. But in conversation with a man like Pauli he receives much more. He gains the assurance of a community of interests, even a community of destiny, which, in the present state of the world, appears under the guise of a common *nostalgia*.

From the end of the eighteenth century, there has arisen a dichotomy—inevitable, to be sure, but nevertheless a little saddening—between a *scientific* interpretation of the world that looks for *laws and principles* regardless of *meanings*; and a *humanistic* interpretation of the world that gropes for *meanings* while no longer being able to believe in *laws* and *principles*. This was not so when both the sciences and the humanities came into being and walked hand in hand for a few glorious centuries. The great historians before Niebuhr and Ranke were not quite satisfied until the *meanings*, which they read into the events, seemed to exemplify some kind of *law or principle*. The great astronomers before Herschel and Laplace were not quite satisfied until their *laws and principles* seemed to reveal some kind of *meaning*.

One of my fondest recollections in connection with our Laureate is the picture of his wistful face when he once mentioned, in the woods behind the Institute, how much impressed he had been by a re-reading of Kepler. Kepler had rectified the distances between the planets and the sun; but he was not really happy—he says so himself—until he discovered that these distances *meant* something. "Playing with symbols"— as he expressed it, much to the disgust of Laplace—he found that the distances could be expressed by the radii of spheres inscribed within or circumscribing five Platonic solids developed with the orbit of the earth as basic unit ("for otherwise," he says, "I would not know why there should be six planets rather than twenty or a hundred"). When, after the discoveries of the *Astronomia Nova*, this series proved to be in- adequate, Kepler formulated—by way of intuition, trial and error rather than by way of deduction—his famous Third Law, "the squares of the periods of revolution are to each other as are the cubes of the distances from the sun," which made him drunk with happiness,—not so much because it was true, as because it accounted not only for the *dimensions* but also for the *motion* of the celestial "spheres," and thus permitted him to see, and to hear, the total harmony of the universe—the same total harmony which, in different form and on an altogether different basis, had been revealed by the "finger of God" to the thought of Ptolemy and Pythagoras. And even this would not have set Kepler's mind at rest had he not known for certain that the ideal center of his new universe—an "empty" center, no longer occupied by either the earth or the sun, but perpetually projecting itself to every single point of the periphery through an infinite number of radii—mirrored or "adumbrated" God the Father unendingly begetting the Son through the Holy Ghost: had he not known for certain that the whole world was one great image of the Trinity.

"This kind of thing has been lost," said Pauli, or words to that effect. Needless to say, we cannot go back. We cannot revert to the acceptance of either classical tradition or Christian dogma, however much revered, as something that guarantees meaning to the laws of nature, and, at the same time, guarantees the force of a law to the meaning of history.

It is with this in mind that a humanist, however small, may greet a scientist, however great, as a *colleague*.

97 Battle Road
Princeton, New Jersey
December 25, 1945

Dear Mr. Tarkington,

I am, not for the first time, embarrassed by your kindness. Here I am, empty-handed (for, the Princeton Press is still so clogged up with its unexpected atomic best-seller that I have long ago given up even asking about the fate of Suger), and "in receipt" of another box of your wonderful cigarettes the very fragrance of which evokes the memory of The Floats and all The Floats stand for. So there is nothing to do but to thank you very much indeed, and to wish you a very good New Year. We had, surprisingly, an almost merry Christmas, with our children, one grandchild, numerous friends, and even my dog dropping in and gathering around a table which gave a very true though not altogether flattering picture of my "system of values": apart from your cigarettes, there was mostly food (among other delicacies a can of cherries grown in the direct vicinity of the Plutonium plant in the State of Washington and, we devoutly hope, no longer radioactive), several bottles of *genuine* Burgundy, two detective stories, two books with drawings and photographs of dogs, one arthistorical treatise and, as the only more spiritual feature, a record of Mozart's earlier concert[o] in E-Flat Major. The nicest present, however, was a letter from one of my young friends in Germany who reported that he had been able to deliver our first packages, one of them containing the much-needed vitamins, to Dora's sister in Berlin, and that this sister herself had been not only reinstated but promoted to Associate Justice in the "Kammergericht" which once decided the famous law-suit between Frederick the Great and the miller Arnold and found against the King; her position corresponds to that of an Associate Justice of the Supreme Court of Massachusetts, or so; but this will unfortunately not restore her health although it entails a higher ration card.

In sum, then, looking back upon 1945, we have a good deal to be thankful for; and, first of all, for so much friendship and loyalty that we can never hope to deserve them. We can only give you our most fervent wishes for a fruitful and, let us hope, peaceful New Year and many more to come.

Yours as ever devotedly,
Erwin Panofsky

Dear Dr. Panofsky:

Betty made copies of the account you sent of the Phila. meeting and we use them (privately) where we think they'll be helpful. Also I refer—not by name—to the Idiot's agreeable plan (40,000,000 of us killed the first day) in a broadcast to this region on the 30th (this month). We'll send you a copy. I'm most grateful for your elegant condensation of the meeting.

Four of the soldiers in our family have returned, two Majors, a Captain, and a Sergeant. One of the Majors, my nephew and namesake, after 42 months abroad, India, Middle East, N. Africa, Sicily, England, France, can't be made to talk of *anything* seriously. The other Major, 52, is gloomy about everything and believes that neither we nor other peoples will abate "sovereignty" enough to save civilization. The Captain and Sergeant, both much younger, say that nations must and will unite to save posterity.

The Sergeant (Military Gov't) was in charge of two German criminal prisons and sorted out the prisoners; put 'em into classes, or types, Most of them had been set free by the confusion but they didn't go far—came back for food and shelter. He's a gentle young man and thought that most of the Nazi guards and the prisoners who were Nazis held him in cold contempt. When he was kind—or no more than fair—they were haughty with him. He'd tried hard to "understand the Germans" but finds them insoluable riddles. I said tritely, "Aren't we all?" and he worriedly assented.

We don't yet know just what the "Big 3" agreement is. I'm apprehensive that "giving it to U. N. O." means only an agreement not to *use* it—a type of blackballing. They may rule out some of the rockets, etc. too—war to *be*, of course, but under the Marquis of Queensbury rules—no gouging, no kicking, just

good clean killing, and armies larger than ever. Heaven
forgive me, I believe this is what the military bureaux
and generals *want*! Also there's the argument that it
avoids "loss of sovereignty." I hope I'm wrong and
that the U. N. O. will work out an international peace
enforcement police duty. At a stag party (my first in
17 years) the day before Christmas, I talked with a
keen chap, middle-aged, just out of the Navy Dept.,
a lawyer previously in one of the best firms here. He
said: "The Washington point-of-view is completely
a conviction and a policy. The government and
the departments are solidly in agreement upon it
and nowhere do you hear even argument about it.
It is this: The war is *over*. It has become history and
efficiency requires that we now *forget* it. All of our
thinking and energy must now be bent upon prepara-
tion for the *next* war." My friend, himself, was strongly
of a different way of thinking; but he said that nobody
could make any impression on "Washington" by
argument against its settled and self-entrenched
position.

Our own returned soldiers (the "family" ones)
say "No" to "Washington." They seem to know their
G. I.'s and this is how they report them: "They, more
than anybody, want peace; they couldn't bear the
thought that this may happen again. What they
want to hear is a *concrete* plan—a chart that anybody
can understand and that will be a Law of Nations
enforcing peace from now on." The Captain and
the Sergeant, who were close to the "rank and file,"
are most earnest about this. The Captain had held talk
sessions with his 250 men—meetings in which everybody had part in discussion—they were unanimous,
he says.

Truman, the State, Army, Navy etc. Depts. all
believe in the "Next War"—the people have to put
up the opposition through Congress. I think Truman's

proved his lack of imagination: he wanted to keep the A-Bomb a "secret," believed it *could* be, still wants peacetime conscription, etc. Seems to be a small, dry mind, a grooved one. His doubt of U. N. O. is expressed in his appointment of delegates, especially Mrs. Roosevelt who will be a great time-waster. Too many of the others will be like her—or like [Harold] Stassen at San Francisco—platitudinizing about the causes of war, bad drainage in Bombay, etc. We can hope, though, that there will emerge one or two practical minds with powers of communication; they could bring about the great decision.

We are not reconciled to the superseding of Suger by Smyth; best-sellers do dreadful things in a publisher's office. I'm fascinated by a wondering— What would Suger have made of it? He knew about "Greek Fire" of course and may have wished that the heathen would agree not to use it.

All the best New Year wishes there are to you and Mrs. Panofsky and, as Rip Van Winkle said, "to all your families."

Affly,

N. B. T.

Tarkington's Lady Hamilton and Her Nelson, *a propaganda radio play written in 1940, did not appear in print until November, 1945, when The House of Books published a limited edition. The radio address referred to is "Fools Will Burn." Tarkington wrote it for the Indiana Committee for Victory in September, 1945.*

"Huff-Duff" was the Army-Navy-Coast Guard word for "high-frequency direction finder," a radio device used during the war to spot lost planes or vessels. It was particularly effective against Axis submarines.

Einstein's assistant at this time was Ernst 121
Straus, a mathematician who came to the In-
stitute for Advanced Study from New York City.

97 Battle Road
Princeton, New Jersey
Dear Mr. Tarkington, January 16, 1946

I should have thanked you before for the precious
gift of your "Lady Hamilton" to Dora (rightly or not,
I consider myself a secondary beneficiary), and for your
admirable radio address. It sums up *all* that which can
reasonably be said about the possibility of warding
off disaster and does it with a force not paralleled
even by your own earlier addresses and essays on the
Atomic Situation. I showed it to Einstein's assistant
and his nice wife who dropped in for some music
the other day, and they were so fascinated by the first
paragraphs that they took it away from me at once,
and I have not seen it since. So I suppose it now
circulates among the physicists and mathematicians,
and this is as it should be. The trouble is that reasonable people only can be convinced by reason, and
therefore don't need convincing so much to begin
with; whereas the less reasonable majority is apt to be
convinced by unreason rather than anything else—
especially when they are misled by seemingly
authoritative pronouncements such as the latest
revelation of the Navy concerning "Huff-Duff" which,
so far as I can see, is "Hum-Bug" if advertised as a
defense against Atomic Bombs; it is said to "either
deflect or to explode" radio-controlled missiles. The
latter is patently untrue in the case of *atomic* missiles;
the former *may* be feasible, but then there arises
the question—a "question to be asked"—deflect where-
to? If the bomb is successfully "deflected" from New

York it might land in Boston instead; and the perfected model may still do considerable harm to Chicago even if successfully "deflected" to the middle of Lake Michigan.

To revert to the beginning: I should, and would have thanked you earlier; but I had to set out on my great venture to Cincinnati; and, apart from the feeling of frustration caused by the unattainability of Indianapolis, it was a really charming experience. It is a very beautiful city, looking almost like something on the Rhine or lower Rhone, and the Taft museum, where I had to hold forth, and where a truly magnificent tea restored the spirits of all concerned, is a perfectly charming mansion of about 1840 (or so it looks), containing some very fine pictures (Gainsborough, Goya, Sargent etc.), lots of Limousine enamels and Renaissance fayence, genuine "period" furniture, and a whole staircase frescoed (or, rather, seccoed) with romantic landscapes by an American painter of about 1850. The whole affair was further blessed by the invisible presence of yourself; for, mine host, the Chairman of the inviting organization was that nice Mr. Moulinier whom I met on the Floats, and among those present were Mr. and Mrs. Black, likewise of cherished Kennebunkportian memory. Thus much of the conversation was centered around the Floats, and all the Floats stand for, and everybody wishes to be respectfully remembered to you. There were, also, some younger people of charm and intelligence, and, on the whole, I have seldom seen such a fine combination of good food, good drink, good company, and good talk. Also, Mr. Moulinier showed me a miniature of a collateral ancestor of his (about 1820, from the style) on which there hangs a tale which sounds half like Balzac and half like Flaubert. The ancestor, a Quaker, had been sent to Russia on some business and fallen in love with a

young Russian girl, and she with him. So they were
married after fierce opposition on either side. But
the young man, having a weak heart not diagnosed
at the time, died on the day after the wedding—
whereupon the young widow, for no apparent reason
except her longing to be where he belonged, packed
up her possessions, icons and all, and went to Philadelphia, where she spent the comparatively short rest
of her life amidst the Quakers (but, so far as I know,
without formal conversion) and never married anyone
else. What a theme!

Princeton is plodding along *more solito*. The
campus is all but impassable, partly on account of the
perambulations of the married G. I.s, partly on account
of the excavations for the iceberg Library. But that is,
thus far, all that is worth reporting.

With our very best wishes for you, Mrs. Tarkington,
Betty and Figaro,
as ever devotedly yours,
Erwin Panofsky

[Indianapolis
February, 1946]

Dear Dr. Panofsky:

I've been waiting pretty long to send you the enclosed generous missive—a pressed-for ms and other
things, mainly sleep, interfering. The book is "No
Ship Shall Sail," a sea-and-Salem historical novel,
and though there are bits of sailorish talk in it, I find
it most uncommonly pure. Nevertheless, it is a pleasure
to know anybody so sensitive to unrefinement as is
your former valet de chambre, weather prophet,
and autobiographarian. Needless to say, his mode
of addressing me caused a stoppage—one in myself
as my eye paused there and refused to go farther
for several minutes. The letter was postmarked
Boston, and I could not imagine WHO, in all that

particular city, would call me "Dearest Friend." If Bostonians have 'em they don't say so.

We are wondering what you think may be the effect of the navy's experiment upon battleships etc. I confess to some uneasiness. It is possible that the *concussion* may leave the ships afloat and that propaganda could thus be encouraged to sound the "just-another-weapon" argument? The fact that no organic life could withstand the bomb might be obscured? Do you know who, among the physicists, are to be present? Don't bother to answer my questions until you have an otherwise indisposable half-hour; but please add the information that you survive the winter robustly and that Mrs. Panofsky is heartily, now, herself again.

As for us here, we are well and (when awake) rather busy. Betty, however, is in a condition of embarrassment because a Public Relations lady (for our Civic Theatre) is determined that the author of the dramatization of "Alice Adams" shall have greatness thrust upon her in the newspapers. Betty isn't used to it and relieves herself with reliefs. This is an atrocious joke, meaning she is now finishing two extremely good low-relief profile portraits of an aged cousin of mine and [of] me.

> Our best to you and all of yours,
> Affly,
> NBT

For eleven months after VJ-Day, Congress debated the military, scientific, and international aspects of atomic energy. Throughout the winter of 1945, Tarkington and Panofsky watched and waited. In this last letter exchanged between them, they shared their fears (and for good rea-

sons) that Congress would not wrest control from the hands of the military.

On November 5, 1945, the House Military Affairs Committee had reported the War Department's May-Johnson Bill calling for the establishment of an Atomic Energy Commission of nine part-time members empowered to select a full-time Administrator. The scientists who had chafed under General Groves feared a military man would be put in charge. On November 27, Senator Brien McMahon and his Special Committee on Atomic Energy opened hearings on the general problems a commission would have to face, and within a month had, with strong backing from President Truman, introduced a bill advocating a civilian board of five full-time members in order to foster further research and development of atomic energy by our scientists. The lines were drawn, and debate continued throughout the spring of 1946. It was August 1 before the McMahon Bill finally passed both Houses and became Public Law 79-585. David E. Lilienthal, then Chairman of the Tennessee Valley Authority, became the first Director of the Atomic Energy Commission. The other members, contrary to Panofsky's predictions, were Lewis L. Strauss, Robert F. Bacher, William W. Waymack, and Sumner T. Pike.

97 Battle Road
Princeton, New Jersey
February 22, 1946

Dear Mr. Tarkington,

I have delayed my answer to some extent because I was trying to find an answer to your very pertinent question as to the possible survival of human beings—

or dogs—on such vessels as may survive, mechanically, the concussion of an atomic bomb dropped into the water. I am sorry to say that I could not find out any positive fact because the whole thing is, of course, surrounded with the usual fanfare of secrecy. The obvious thing is, of course, to equip each vessel with one of those highly developed registering instruments ("Geiger counters" etc.) which permit a subsequent reading of the amount of radiation received, and this would give a very exact idea of what *would* have happened had a human being—or dog—been exposed to the same amount (cf. p. 11 ff. in the enclosed publication of the talks delivered in Philadelphia which, I hope, will be of interest to you also in other respects since it includes the very informative talks by Oppenheimer, Langmuir, and—at a considerable distance—Viner). The problem is, of course, to what extent the results will be published. The Navy will probably triumphantly announce that 20 vessels out of, say, 60 "came through with flying colors" but— assuming such to be the case—neglect to mention the fact that the human—and canine—complement of these vessels would have been horribly dead 16 hours later.

The whole thing becomes worse and worse since the Canadian spy scare—released a whole year after the fact when Mr. Truman has good reasons to keep people's eyes off the bill, and when the generals have still better reasons to defeat the McMahon Bill. We have all been frantically telegraphing our Senators and Congressmen in favor of McMahon and received the usual polite equivocations; but the odds are that the bill finally passed will be *either* the May-Johnson Bill with some slight concessions to the scientists*

---

* such as the dismissal of the Idiot and/or the introduction of a *civilian* Board

or the McMahon Bill with so many amendments in favor of the military that the difference will not matter very much. The only hope is that bills as such—like all legislation—are unimportant in comparison with the persons applying them (Germany had the best constitution in the world from 1914 to 1932 and yet went Nazi because the people applied the laws in a manner conducive thereto). But even this hope is dim in the present situation; even assuming the "Supreme Board" were to be composed of civilians, even scientists, instead of military gentlemen, the leading "civilians" would probably be [James B.] Conant of Harvard and Vannevar Bush of M. I. T. who are, in reality, *more* militaristic than the generals themselves—much as Mr. Bevin is *more* imperialistic than Churchill. It is interesting, though frightening, to observe how this whole situation poisons the atmosphere in our insitutions of learning, primarily, of course, in the Physics and Chemistry Departments, but secondarily the whole shop. My little son Wolf, for instance, has recently received a very flattering invitation to come to *Princeton,* but he finds it terribly difficult to make up his mind: where he is, he has the apparatus he needs for the problems that are of interest to him but is badgered by the Army—were he to come here he would be a free man and save his soul but would not have the apparatus (which seems to depend on Army material) and would have to start on something for which—or so he thinks—he is less well equipped as an individual researcher. Whatever he does, he will have misgivings (which, of course, would matter very little were not basic science to be the loser in *either* event). *Basic* science, by the way, has been defined by General Groves as "things either known to all or easy to find out." Our only relief was a visit to the very nice Tarkington exhibition (beginning 1893) which our Univ. Library has arranged—as you undoubtedly know. Suger proceeds, fortunately slowly—fortunately, because it was thus possible for me to expunge a terrific boner kindly brought to my attention (though I should have caught it myself) by Mr. Crosby of Yale, who had done excavations and could thus prove that I had placed a door into an absolutely and unalterably solid wall. Now I have put it into a place where no excavation can be started as long as St. Denis exists and feel fairly safe; but I have naturally to confess the whole thing on the *Addenda et Corrigenda* page. This wall, at which I almost hit my theoretician's head, is the most eloquent example of what is known as a "stubborn fact."

I am also enclosing a little atomic play, both witty and terrifying (because of its inherent truthfulness) which I received from Mr. Pauli. He gave me two copies, so please don't bother to return it. I can also do without the Philadelphia *Proceedings* in case they should hold your interest.

With warmest wishes from both of us to all of you,

Yours as ever devotedly,
Erwin Panofsky

Many thanks for the touching letter from Mr. Maling! "Blessed are the pure in heart."

Princeton University Library arranged an exhibition of Booth Tarkington's works in the Treasure Room during the months of March and April, 1946. Erwin Panofsky readily consented to write a preface to the catalogue, not a criticism of the work or a description of the exhibition but an appreciation of the man. Very likely the staff of the Library, as well as the Panofskys, were expecting Tarkington to arrive for the opening.

Unfortunately his last public appearance was March 7 when he attended a performance of Betty Trotter's dramatization of Alice Adams *at the Indianapolis Civic Theater. After only two months' illness, Tarkington died on May 19. What better epilogue could there be to their eight-year correspondence than this affectionate tribute written by the gentleman from Princeton for the gentleman from Indiana?*

HUMANITAS TARKINGTONIANA

KENNEBUNKPORT is an old village on the coast of Maine. In its youth it was a renowned and prosperous seaport and ship-building center, and it is still proud of its ancient harbor, tall elm trees, smooth lawns and unobtrusively dignified eighteenth-century houses. When the visitor wanders down the River to the ocean his eye is arrested by the sight of an old schooner, named "Regina," majestically docked alongside a weather-beaten boat-house that juts out into the tidal waters. Having passed the friendly scrutiny of a former sea-captain who acts as guard, caretaker, steward, occasional cook and permanent carpenter (there is always something to fix in such lacustrine dwellings), the stranger is admitted to the semi-darkness of a long, high room whose varied contents bring to mind the "Kunst und Wunderkammern" of the Baroque; and on a sunlit porch at the far end of this room, overhanging the river, he meets Booth Tarkington.

To meet Booth Tarkington is like meeting a whole period of history. In his long life he has come to know nearly everybody worth knowing, seen nearly everything worth seeing, read nearly everything worth reading, and done nearly everything worth doing. It must have been a similar experience to meet Dr.

130 Johnson—with one essential difference: Dr. Johnson was primarily interested in opinions and only secondarily in those who held them; Booth Tarkington is primarily interested in human beings and only secondarily in what they believe or profess to believe. Instead of respecting a man because he understands his convictions, Booth Tarkington respects a conviction, however much different from his own, because he understands the man.

This passionate humanism is the guiding force in Booth Tarkington's work as well as in his life. It is not an accident that his fine collection of pictures consists very largely of portraits, and that he has dealt with these in a book the like of which no art historian could ever write—a book that compels the painter to tell us more about human nature than he revealed in the picture, and compels the sitter to tell us more about human nature than he revealed to the painter. And as Booth Tarkington looks upon works of art with the psychological interest of the novelist so does he look upon human beings with the loving acquisitiveness of the collector. They attract him as strongly as he attracts them; he treasures them in the glass case of his prodigious memory; he examines them under the sharp yet never distorting lens of his insight and humor; he handles them with the delicate touch of his unfailing courtesy; and, occasionally, he sends a choice specimen to an exhibition by putting it into a story.

In direct contrast to the snob "whose conduct or opinions are influenced by the acceptance of social position or wealth or success" (*Oxford Dictionary*), Booth Tarkington behaves, to quote from Bernard Shaw, "as if he were in Heaven, where there are no third-class carriages, and one soul is as good as another." He tells of his conversations with Theodore Roosevelt or Henry James with no more gusto and real interest than of his encounters with New York art

dealers or Neapolitan *vetturini*. He quotes a witticism
of Mark Twain's much in the same spirit as he quotes
the sayings of his distinguished colored butler (recently
voted "the best-dressed man of Kennebunkport"),
or as he relates the exploits of his native chauffeur
(who was engaged, some thirty years ago, because his
perennial scowl and love of tranquillity prevented
him from being a success as a taxi-driver and who
still considers it loquacious to sound his horn even
when another car is about to back into his own).

Thus the old boat-house on the Kennebunk River
is a curious microcosm, a human universe in a nut-
shell. It is open to gentlemen retired from the
presidency—or the ticket window—of a big railroad,
and to the budding actors and actresses of the local
summer theatre; to friends so old that they remember,
and never tire to recount, the plays performed on
Broadway when New York had just received the blessings of electricity, and to friends so new that they
have to be initiated into the very rudiments of
Kennebunkportian folklore; to students just home
from the war of 1945, and to veterans reminiscing
about the war of 1898. All these men, women and
half-children come to Booth Tarkington with their
memories, hopes and sorrows, confiding in him and
craving his advice. He talks to all of them and listens
to all of them. For he, the best of raconteurs, is also—a
combination almost unique—the best of listeners,
and there is nothing on earth, from the emotional
problems of a freshman to the political problems of
the United Nations, from the technique of Gothic
glass painters to nuclear physics, from an anecdote
about the court of Louis XIV to the way of navigating
a whaling ship, that would not hold his interest and
stimulate his imagination.

All this takes place in the afternoons, over a cup
of very excellent coffee. Booth Tarkington's mornings

and evenings are spent, not in the boat-house but in a seignorial mansion on the hill, the mornings with work, the evenings with reading, music or an occasional dinner party. In the evening the family dresses, and then the tall, frail figure of the master of the house may give to the observer the impression of formality. However, what is formality (meaning: pattern devoid of content) in others is genuine form (meaning: pattern expressive of content) in Booth Tarkington. His dress and manners express respect for his company as well as for convention, and his politeness is not only a *politesse de l'esprit* but also, or rather more so, a *politesse du coeur*. His way of rising at the entrance of any visitor, his way of offering to his guests precisely the chair, the kind of cigarettes and the kind of music that he knows they like—all this flows from the same impulses which reveal themselves, on another level, in an unlimited generosity. It will never be known how many people are indebted to his generosity in financial matters; but no less numerous must be those who are indebted to his generosity in matters of the spirit. It is, in general, sadly true that illness and age make men self-centered. Booth Tarkington, who has gone through many an illness and is now nearly seventy-seven, appears to be more rather than less concerned about his fellow-beings. I know of men and women who might not have survived a crisis of suspense and despair had not Booth Tarkington fortified them with the strength of his understanding and sympathy.

A deep respect for humanity is also at the bottom of his political convictions. Booth Tarkington is a conservative and would probably not even mind being called a Tory. But he is not a reactionary. When he disapproves of the New Deal he regrets, and has some reason to regret, the disappearance of certain human types, human attitudes, human relations, and human values that he cherishes; he fears a loss of freedom where others merely fear a loss of privilege. It is therefore no more than consistent that the same man who fairly and squarely opposed Franklin Delano Roosevelt for many years acclaimed him as a maker of war against tyranny; and that he devoted to him an obituary more just, more moving and more sincere than many others. It is no more than consistent that the same man who objects to socialization objects, and no less vigorously, to conscription and military control of atomic energy. When it comes to *dignitas hominis*—a concept, after all, of fairly ancient origin— there is perhaps as little difference between a true conservative and a true liberal as there may be between a reactionary and a "progressive."

Erwin Panofsky